T0163288

Published by Periplus Editions (HK) Ltd.

www.periplus.com

Copyright © 1998 Periplus Editions (HK) Ltd.

All rights reserved.

ISBN: 978-962-593-100-5
LCC Number 97069546

Distributed by

North America, Latin America & Europe
Tuttle Publishing
364 Innovation Drive
North Clarendon, VT 05759-9436 U.S.A.
Tel: 1 (802) 773-8930
Fax: 1 (802) 773-6993
info@tuttlepublishing.com
www.tuttlepublishing.com

Japan
Tuttle Publishing
Yaekari Building 3rd Floor
5-4-12 Osaki
Shinagawa-ku Tokyo 141 0032
Tel: (81) 3 5437-0171
Fax: (81) 3 5437-0755
sales@tuttle.co.jp
www.tuttle.co.jp

Asia Pacific
Berkeley Books Pte. Ltd.
3 Kallang Sector #04-01
Singapore 349278
Tel: (65) 6741 2178
Fax: (65) 6741 2179
inquiries@periplus.com.sg
www.tuttlepublishing.com

Acknowledgments
The publisher gratefully acknowledges the assistance of the following people in the preparation of this book: Jean-Luc Maumus, chef Greg Picolo, and the entire staff of The Bistro and the Hotel Maison de Ville; chef Dominique Macquet, who was instrumental in the preparation of the food for photography; Dinah and Rich Laurich of Bay Tree Plantation; Mrs. Ong for her invaluable help with props and logistical support during the photo shoot; Vaughn Schmitt of Creole Country, John Abernathy and Donald Welty of Carriage Foods, Bubba Scott of Bubba's Produce Company, and Donna Patrick of Inland Seafood; and the many New Orleans chefs and shop owners who generously contributed to the book. The publisher also wishes to thank Mr. Patrick Robert, guide extraordinaire, for his fascinating introduction to the River Road and its many notable sights.

Photo Credits
All food photographs by John Hay. Additional photos by: John Hay, p. 3; Syndey Byrd, pp. 2, 12–19, 22–24, 26; Alex Demyan, p. 25; Frank Lotz Miller, p. 1-. Watercolor page 6 (detail) by Boyd Cruise; photograph page 8 by Charles L. Franck Photographers; photograph on page 9 by Charles Genella, and images on pages 1 and 7 are reproduced courtesy of the Williams Research Center, The Historic New Orleans Collection.

Behind the Scenes
The making of this book was a labor of love for our entire creative team. Each book in the World Foods series strives for authenticity in every sense of the word. This meant, first of all, finding the best chefs and gathering the best recipes in all of New Orleans. It meant getting expert New Orleans-based writers who know the city's cuisine inside and out. It meant gathering the most beautiful objects on which to serve the food. And it meant shooting each dish on location in the city's best restaurants, among curious diners and bustling waiters, or carting gallons of boiled seafood to create the ultimate picnic on the rolling lawns of a Louisiana plantation. We've emerged from this creative whirlwind with a thorough appreciation for the food, music, and history of this charming city, and we hope you will savor this experience yourself in the pages that follow.

23 22 21 20
17 16 15 14 13

Printed in Singapore   1912TP

THE FOOD OF
NEW ORLEANS

Authentic Recipes from the Big Easy

Text and recipes by John DeMers

With additional articles by Marcelle Bienvenu,
Ella Brennan, Paul A. Greenberg, Errol Laborde, and Honey Naylor

Food photography by John Hay
With additional photography by Syndey Byrd

Styling by Fiona Hammond and Christina Ong

Produced in association with the Hotel Maison de Ville

Featuring recipes from the following New Orleans restaurants

Andrea's	The Cabin
Arnaud's	Commander's Palace
Bayona	Dominique's
The Bistro	K-Paul's Louisiana Kitchen
Brennan's	Mike's on the Avenue
	The Sazerac

PERIPLUS EDITIONS

Singapore • Hong Kong • Indonesia

Contents

Part One: Food in New Orleans

On the foundations of Creole and Cajun cooking, a city builds a temple to terrific food

by John DeMers

Lavishly festooned with magnolia and bougainvillea, New Orleans is an American city unlike any other. This steamy Southern metropolis is well loved for its charming architecture, its music—especially jazz—and its riotous Mardi Gras celebration. Yet most of all, it is revered for its food.

The city's unique history—it was founded by French colonists in the eighteenth century—and location at the mouth of the Mississippi River have given it a personality all its own. Its French roots may be why New Orleanians are known for their love of good food—nowhere else will you find so many famous dishes: gumbo, crawfish étouffée, jambalaya, muffuletta sandwiches—the list goes on.

Situated at the mouth of the largest and most important waterway in America, New Orleans has welcomed immigrants from around the world. And its food reveals the contributions of the city's many peoples—not only the first French and Spanish colonists, the Creoles (descendants of French, Spanish, African, and Caribbean colonists), and the Cajuns (French-Canadian immigrants who arrived in the eighteenth century), but also West Indians, Germans, Italians, Chinese, and Thais, to name a few.

No other American city can boast an unbroken tradition of fine dining as long as that of New Orleans; its classic French cuisine can be sampled in dining rooms that are over 150 years old. At the same time, it's hard to think of any other American city that has undergone such dramatic culinary change in one generation, evolving from a place that once scorned any food not its own into a city that now embraces dishes and cooking techniques from around the world.

This new spirit has reinvigorated New Orleans cuisine, which had become somewhat frozen in time. In recent years the old dynastic restaurant system, in which chefs handed down their recipes from generation to generation, has been challenged by a new breed of eateries built around a single innovative chef-owner's vision. The result has been change, growth, diversity, and excitement.

What New Orleans cuisine is about today is surprise. Just when you expect a classic dish unchanged from its roots, the one put before you could be straight out of the trendiest food magazine—next month's edition, no less. And just when you think these young chefs have gone crazy, out comes the most glorious traditional Creole courtbouillon or Cajun *cochon de lait*. There is no way to predict; there are only ways to enjoy.

This book is about the mystery and magic of New Orleans cooking. It explores the flavors of the city's intermingled cultures, the shifts and slants of its rich history, and its deep spirit of celebration.

Page 2: *Jazz legends Worthia G. Thomas, Frank Frederico, Charles Burbank, Jerry Adams, and Lionel Ferbos epitomize the spirit of New Orleans.* *Opposite*: *No Mardi Gras celebration would be complete without the traditional Red Beans and Rice with Corn Bread. See page 133 for recipes.*

Crescent City Culinary Origins

A brief history of settlers who taught a kitchen to sing

by Honey Naylor

Imagine, if you will, the French or Spanish master of a New Orleans household struggling to teach the kitchen help to prepare his favorite dish. The cook may have been a slave from Africa, or a free person of mixed race, whose cooking experience was based entirely on the preparation of his or her native foods. It was left to the cook to interpret a complicated recipe, in a different language, using new ingredients. Authenticity was irrelevant; getting dinner on the table was all that mattered.

Now imagine these same "European" recipes being taught by slave to freed slave to immigrant, perhaps even someday being taught to a classically trained chef, who probably wouldn't even recognize its buried origins. All that remained of the original was a misspelled word or a questionable reference to a particular technique. What now existed on the plate, what took this chef's breath away, was something entirely new. It was a cuisine born in and for a new world. And it was terrific.

The Creoles of the French Quarter in the 1800s lived comfortably. This watercolor shows Dumaine Street between Dauphine and Bourbon Streets at that time.

There is no moment at which we can say, Look, there it is, the birth of New Orleans cuisine. Every moment in the city's history has been part of this birth, and, truly, the cuisine is constantly being reborn. Every French or Spanish colonist added something to the pot. Every cook added the flavors of his or her own experience. And in their search for the taste of home, each immigrant group—Sicilian, Greek, German, Irish, Croatian, Vietnamese, Thai—added something.

The outside world would give this cooking a name—usually Creole, or out in the countryside, Cajun. But this food is the child of everyone who has ever cooked a meal in New Orleans.

Historians, perhaps grabbing at straws, have come up with one incident that at least symbolically evokes the beginning of New Orleans Creole cuisine. In 1722, in what became known as the Petticoat Rebellion, about fifty young wives marched on Governor Bienville's mansion in New Orleans, pounding their frying pans with metal spoons and protesting their dreary diet of cornmeal mush.

With a dash of admirable dexterity, Bienville put the women in touch with a certain Madame Langlois, who had learned more than a few secrets from the local Choctaw Indians.

It was she who calmed the angry wives by teaching them how to use powdered sassafras for flavor in the gumbo they'd already tasted from the hands of African slaves (*gumbo* being the West African word for *okra*), how to prepare hominy grits, how to squeeze the most flavor (and indeed the greatest variety of meals) from the region's abundant fish (such as trout, red snapper, and the highly prized pompano), shellfish (shrimp, crabs, and crawfish—also called "mudbugs" by locals), and game.

It is not an error to say Creole cooking is French, even though that is a gross oversimplification. The French founded the colony they called La Nouvelle Orleans in 1718, near the mouth of the Mississippi. At that time child-king Louis XV sat on the throne, but France was actually ruled by its regent, Philippe II, Duc d'Orleans. It was for the duke that the new settlement was named. Its first streets were named after French royals of the day.

From the beginning, New Orleans cuisine in-

The famous French Market of New Orleans was so central to the city's culinary life that it even turned up on coffee labels.

corporated a flurry of French words and, at least in certain ways, the flavors of France. There were ravigotes and rémoulades, étouffées and beignets. There was reverence for lush sauces, from béarnaise to hollandaise; butter and cream were used generously. But later generations would scratch their heads at New Orleans recipes, wondering how a dish with a name found back in France looked and tasted so little like its namesake.

Perhaps the richness of the food consoled the colonists through those hard first years—and they needed consolation indeed. Set on the bank of a great crescent in the wide brown river, much of the city lies five feet below sea level, with surrounding swamps and bayous as far as the unhappy eye can see. The colony had to be carved out of thick canebrakes, and the Creoles were forced to battle hurricanes, floods, and yellow fever without rest. New Orleans' penchant for partying may actually stem from those tragic earliest days, when mere survival was cause for celebration.

The first colonists of La Nouvelle Orleans were soon joined by African slaves and then by German settlers. In the mid–eighteenth century, New Orleans came under the control of Spain—introducing a host of new flavors and techniques from Spanish holdings across the Americas, ranging from

Italian fruit vendors in the French Market at the turn of the century.

The port of New Orleans is less than a day's steam from the spot where the Mississippi River meets the Gulf of Mexico. In 1803 the port was a bustling center of trade, and Thomas Jefferson—bent on keeping it out of Napoleon's hands—purchased the entire Louisiana Territory for fifteen million dollars. This single transaction gave the United States a vision of itself that within a handful of years would reach outward to the Pacific Ocean.

Thousands of people rushed to the new American city. By 1840, New Orleans was one of the largest and wealthiest cities in the nation—with restaurants worthy of patrons who wanted to (and could afford to) eat well. Nearly all the places founded then are only memories now. There was Moreau's, reputed to be the best, and a place called Fabacher's, by far the largest. The latter served up to two thousand meals on an average day, as many as five thousand on Mardi Gras—an irony, since most fine dining establishments now lock their doors on Fat Tuesday.

tomatoes to corn to the act of deep-frying itself.

It was during this colonial period that thousands of Acadians (or Cajuns) came to southern Louisiana from present-day Nova Scotia and New Brunswick in Canada. They were descendants of French speakers who, at the dawn of the seventeenth century, colonized those Canadian provinces—only to be driven out and down the coast by the British.

This was also when New Orleans suffered two devastating fires; the rebuilt city we see today reflects a decidedly Spanish flavor, resembling Old San Juan more than it does Paris, Rouen, or Nice. After the turn of the nineteenth century, Spain let Louisiana slip back to France, but the French flag flew over the colony for only twenty days.

Begue's was a Creole landmark near the French Market, famed for its gargantuan breakfasts of seafoods, meats, and wines that could last up to four hours. New Orleans' oldest surviving restaurant, the world-famous Antoine's, started out as a humble boardinghouse.

Today, New Orleans is a diversified commercial and tourist center, yet its riverfront is still a significant component of the economy. It has extensive dock facilities along the river and along man-made shortcuts like the Gulf Intracoastal Waterway and the Mississippi River Gulf Outlet. Exports from New Orleans' vast hinterland include grains, cotton, and petroleum products. Crawfish and catfish production are also important industries, and Louisiana is known for the quality of its rice, sweet potatoes, sugar cane, strawberries, and tomatoes.

Despite some nods to the twentieth century—a proliferation, for instance, of high-rise, high-tech convention hotels—New Orleans still has a foot firmly planted in the past.

New Orleans is anything but a neat, orderly city, and therein lies part of its charm, as well as its great appeal to writers and artists. The French Quarter, one of the city's ten historic districts, is carefully preserved, right down to its peeling paint and cracked flagstones. It is a lively living museum, a business center, and even a residential district, as well as the city's primary tourist attraction.

If you stop in the Quarter near the Vieux Carré for beignets and a cup of chicory-laced coffee, you will be near the site of the original colony of La Nouvelle Orleans, with the same boundaries today as when it was first laid out by French engineers in the eighteenth century.

Beignets and café au lait have been a New Orleans pleasure since the 1800s.

The city cherishes its French heritage and loves its legends of voodoo queens and grinning buccaneers. Yet we also take pride in the fact that New Orleans is the first American city in which opera was performed. For the most part, day in and night out, New Orleans is mindful of those qualities that make it unique—on the street or on the plate. We take pride in our food, our music, and our fun; and we wake up each day inviting the world to join us.

Growing Up with Great Food

*The grande dame of New Orleans' first family of food
remembers the flavors of her childhood*

by Ella Brennan

As children growing up in New Orleans, we had an extraordinary culinary experience, and we didn't even know it. We thought everybody else in the world had a mother who was just as good a cook as ours. She was a wonderful cook. And with six children around the table, meals were always a happy time. She spoiled us with good food.

My mother was an intuitive cook, like many women and men here in New Orleans. I remember following her around as a child. She had magic in her hands. Now I say that all great cooks have magic in their hands, and she certainly did. There was nothing complicated about this, believe me. It was the simplest thing she could do.

She didn't have to prepare for weeks or go to the grocery store with a list. She had a pantry that she kept stocked. And meats, poultry, seafood, the freshest vegetables and fruits anyone could ever want— these were part of our lives as kids, right along with the people who prepared them for us at the little

John, Dottie, and Dick Brennan (standing, from left) and Ella and Adelaide Brennan (seated), founders of Commander's Palace.

markets or delivered them to our door. Sometimes it's the people I remember even more than the food—but that's okay because who can separate them, anyway?

My mother had a butcher, Mr. Manale, who brought her meat. She had a fish person. The vegetable man, Mr. Tony, came to the front door. The banana man, the milkman, the coffee man—they all came right to our house back then, and they were my mother's friends.

As kids, we got to know them. Mr. Tony used to drive us to school on occasion. These people would always be in the kitchen, having a cup of coffee, having a glass of iced tea. Our house was food-oriented, but we didn't realize it until many years later.

There was a bakery across the street from our school. When my brother Dick was little, I had to go pick him up after his classes. And we'd be throwing the bread back and forth between us all the way home because it was so hot.

My mother's brothers used to fish and hunt all the time. They would always bring back the things they'd caught for her to prepare. I can still hear them whistling as they came through the door, bringing my mother the freshest redfish imaginable. I decided long ago that there's no better dish on earth than my mother's baked redfish with Creole sauce. It was a very light sauce: fresh tomatoes, onions, and green peppers, served with white rice. We were Irish, not French, but my mother was New Orleans.

When we first got into the restaurant business, we were very fortunate to have some wonderful people to help us out. They were all much older than we were, and these kitchen guys adopted us. We spent hours just sitting with them learning. We shared books with them, and they shared books with us.

From its beginning, Creole cuisine has been experimental. It evolved with French settlers modifying their traditional recipes to the produce of the New World. Based on adaptation and innovation, it has been a cuisine of intuition, with recipes often not written down and no hard-and-fast rules. Sometimes in New Orleans there are as many recipes for a dish as there are cooks.

The Brennan family, whose members— gathered here for Christmas—have founded many of New Orleans' best-loved restaurants.

All this has been true at Commander's Palace since we started here. Truth is, I don't like working with people who aren't growing. I don't want to work with people who are satisfied being where they are. I say if it's not broken, let's break it. There's always a better way.

The good New Orleans restaurateur takes and pulls this creative energy out of people. We Brennans didn't know we had it in us, but people pulled it out of us, and here we are. Now we try to pull it out of others. We try to get people to soar.

This Ethnic Gumbo Pot

New Orleans cooking is the product of more than two centuries of immigration

by Paul A. Greenberg

Right: *Local entertainer Frogman Henry takes a quintessential New Orleans lunch break with a softshell crab po-boy on Bourbon Street.* **Opposite:** *Enticing muffuletta sandwiches on the counter of the Central Grocery in the French Quarter. Only a tourist would order a whole one; natives know that half is more than enough.*

They came by the thousands from lands of desperation to streets they had heard were paved with gold. With dreams of prosperity and fortune, they came from Africa, Ireland, France, Spain, Italy, Sicily, Croatia, Germany, and everyplace in between.

When the immigrants arrived in New Orleans throughout the eighteenth and nineteenth centuries, they brought their cooking styles, their seasonings, and their tastes with them. And over time these influences have merged to become contemporary New Orleans cuisine.

It was as if a giant stew cooked over an open, raging fire for a hundred years, with people of varying skin colors, languages, and rituals taking turns stirring the pot. In the end, there was gumbo—the very real Creole-Cajun dish, and the equally real metaphor for everything New Orleanians love to eat.

Native American herbs and spices, combined with cooking artistry of the culinary triumvirate—French, Spanish, and African settlers—begat Creole cooking. But the true beauty of Creole came

from the inclusion of all arriving cultures. West Indians added more peppers and allspice and even new vegetables, such as mirlitons, which continue to grace New Orleanian tables. The Haitians knew how to add just enough bitters and brandy to startle the long-established French palate.

If the French represented the epitome of refinement in cooking and the lusty West Indians the barefoot contributors of seasoning, someone had to take the middle ground. Fleeing from famine, pestilence, and government upheavals came the Germans, the Italians, and the long-suffering Irish.

The potato famine that began in mid–nineteenth century Ireland sent tens of thousands of Irish to America. Their potato and cabbage heritage traveled with them, as did their love for eggs, baked bread, stews, and big, fresh vegetables. The Irish make their influence felt every day in New Orleans.

The Germans had just as immediate a reason to flee their homeland. The Napoleonic Wars in the Rhine Valley prompted a mass exodus to America,

and New Orleans was the destination of choice for many of them. Even when the war subsided, Germans continued to flow into the port city during a two-year famine in the Rhineland. Most could not afford the passage to America, so they struck deals with Dutch shippers. They agreed to work for up to eight years as indentured servants in America in exchange for transportation. By 1910 they constituted the largest single foreign-born group in New Orleans.

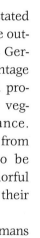

St. Patrick's Day, March 17, is a rowdy festival day for the city's Irish community.

Their poverty dictated that they settle on the outskirts of the city. The Germans took full advantage of their location and produced fresh, plump vegetables in abundance. They sold their crops from trucks and came to be known for their colorful array of produce and their hearty dispositions.

Eventually the Germans opened restaurants. New Orleanians were introduced to many different kinds of sausages (including braunschweiger, blutwurst, leberwurst) and delicacies such as potato dumplings, apple streusel, and always, on every table, big, frothy pitchers of beer. By the mid–nineteenth century, the Germans were laying the groundwork for New Orleans to become a premier brewing center.

As was the case with so many other cultures that came to America, Italians had left their homeland only because they had to. Famines and widespread epidemics forced mid–nineteenth-century Italians to this country—and to New Orleans, a city with a climate they were used to and with a familiar French and Spanish population. The Italian population became known for the fresh fruits they grew and sold. Classic Italian foods are still abundantly served throughout the city. But the single most lasting culinary contribution the Italians made was the muffuletta sandwich.

In 1900 Salvatore Lupo, proprietor of the Central Grocery in the French Quarter, developed a custom of giving Italian farmers a small dish of mixed olive salad along with some salami, cheese, and a piece of round bread known in Lupo's native Sicily as muffuletta. The farmers would awkwardly balance all the separate spicy components on their knees, as was their way in Sicily.

The conversations at the Central Grocery were lively debates punctuated with lots of passionate gesturing. It would often happen that a bowl of olive salad would crash to the concrete floor while someone else's salami would fly through the air—all for the sake of getting a point across.

Sometimes a farmer would stand and wildly shake his fist in the air as he spoke, waving his wedge of cheese.

One day, weary of sweeping up salami and olive salad from the floor, Lupo offered the farmers all the ingredients *inside* the muffuletta, which he had split in half. Little did Lupo know that the sandwich he had invented for his own convenience, this new-fangled concoction, would become as much a part of New Orleans culture as gumbo. Now muffulettas are also filled with ingredients like soft-shell crab.

Perhaps the best example of immigrant innovation was the development of the oyster industry by the Croatians, known for most of this century as Yugoslavs. So determined were they to succeed in this country that they gave up almost everything in their lives except work.

Typically, the oyster grower doomed himself to a life of hard labor from dawn until well after dark every day. The Croatians handled the oyster business around New Orleans in a highly organized fashion between the mid–1800s and the 1950s, albeit with the assistance of machines by then. Today, the fisheries around New Orleans gather twenty percent of the nation's oyster crop.

The number of Asian restaurants in New Orleans speaks to the breadth of culinary influence of the Chinese, Japanese, Koreans, and Thais. When the U.S. government chose New Orleans as a settling point for thousands of Vietnamese expatriates, the city became the willing recipient of yet another culture's knowledge and artistry with food.

The aged streets of New Orleans are home to some of the world's finest restaurants. And the names of some of the most established eateries tell the unique multicultural tale of New Orleans.

It is a rich tale, spiced with names like Garcia, Gio-

Cajun settlers from Nova Scotia and New Brunswick brought their music to the bayous when they migrated from Canada. Cajun and Zydeco music are increasingly popular throughout the United States.

vanni, Barreca, Uglesich, and Fong. Meals are served throughout the city by Clancy, Fitzgerald, Tandoor, and Figaro. These are the streets of Jaeger, O'Brien, Lafitte, Manale, Mosca, Reginelli, O'Henry, Igor, and Vucinovich.

These streets have the fragrant aroma of foods with a history of labor, love, and acculturation—mixed with the profound scent and good sense of America's true melting pot.

The Culture That Feeds Us

From kingcakes to Jazzfest, New Orleans is a festival of food

by Errol Laborde

As the days count down to Mardi Gras in New Orleans, it's not enough to be king (or queen!) for the day. The tongue-in-cheek ascension to twenty-four-hour royalty must by accompanied by a festive food—in this case, the kingcake, a sweeter-than-heaven cousin to the French brioche. Before there's truth (the message seems to be), and even before there's meaning, there's a food to give it form.

No one can count the number of ways that food gives purpose and pleasure to just plain getting by in New Orleans. Mealtime becomes, by definition, festival time. Yet to truly understand how and why New Orleans food is what it is and does what it does, you must observe this unique culture in action.

You must observe carefully, though. Anything less produces the standard-issue image of the brain-dead party town bingeing its way into the morning light. This conception is a terrible affront not only to the food of New Orleans but to the millions of New Orleanians who have transmuted life's joys and sorrows into something that touches the infinite, something that might be defined as that rarity: realistic happiness.

In the weeks before Mardi Gras (a time defined as Carnival, beginning with the Christian observance of Twelfth Night and climaxing on Fat Tuesday itself), variations on Europe's kingcake have become plentiful. This sugar-coated confection, served at parties and office coffee breaks throughout Carnival season, is as rich in ingredients as it is in legend.

One slice always contains an object, most often a small plastic doll. The person who draws that slice becomes, depending on the setting, the king or queen for the moment—at least until the next party, when another cake is served. "Let them eat cake" is not an insult from royalty here; in New Orleans it can be one of the ways of achieving royalty.

As a matter of geography and government, New Orleans is very much an American city. But to understand New Orleans properly, you have to realize that in terms of culinary innovation, as well as

Opposite:
Too many chefs can't spoil this five-thousand-egg omelet in Abbeville.
Left: *Stirring the big pot at the Gumbo Festival.*

character and personality, it is more than just American—and more than just a city.

In many ways New Orleans is an island, with the river winding along one side, Lake Pontchartrain and its marshes on another, and the Gulf of Mexico to the south. Like an island, it tends to have a style of its own, including its own dialect and distinctive modes of celebration.

In some ways, New Orleans might even be considered to be the northernmost island of the Caribbean. As in most Caribbean spots, there is a black majority but a European heritage and white economic power.

Like the Caribbean, New Orleans also has a native music form, a tradition of Carnival celebrations, poverty alongside a wealthy social class, voodoo, and a form of cooking that is hot and spicy. See New Orleans and, in many ways, you see the New World.

Festivals are thrown for any number of reasons, like this one devoted to shrimp and petroleum. Here, the Knights of Columbus and their wives eat shrimp aboard a shrimp boat.

See New Orleans and you're also likely to see some type of celebration, probably one reflecting different parts of the world. Festivals, in general, reign all year in New Orleans.

First and foremost, there is Mardi Gras. The most visual manifestation of the season is the parade. Less visible, but very much a part of the cultural entwining of the city, is a series of Carnival balls, debutante cotillions, and parties, many with their own royalty. Carnival can be as simple as a parade or as deep and anthropological as its pagan roots, its Christian symbolism, and social stratification.

The world embraces the Carnival season's last day—a movable date tailored by Christianity in order to lend some religious significance to the pagan tendency to celebrate the arrival of spring. The Catholic Church gave the celebration a spot on the calendar and a message: a blowout before the onset of fasting. Fasting, in New Orleans, is a passionate form of eating; it focuses both stomach and mind on the next noteworthy meal.

New Orleans, founded by the French, adopted Mardi Gras with enthusiasm. Ironically, as the church became more lax about its rules for Lenten sacrifice, the city began to experience the best of both worlds. The city became adept at the feasting without the fasting.

Next to Mardi Gras, the biggest celebration is the New Orleans Jazzfest, which is spread over two weekends in late April and early May. Unlike Carnival, at which celebrants prefer liquid nourishment punctuated by the simplest fried chicken or smoked sausage, Jazzfest is about cuisine. As its full name, the New Orleans Jazz and Heritage Festival, implies, this gathering is devoted to anything and everything that defines a people—which in New Orleans means music, art, and plenty of food.

A highlight of any Jazzfest day is strolling through the rows of food booths serving up Creole, Cajun, soul, African, Caribbean, and just about any other cuisine that ever crossed paths with New Orleans. You can't expect all the tastes to get along perfectly in your mouth, but you can expect them to get along—a mirror of New Orleans in more ways than one.

Yet for all the flavors of Carnival and Jazzfest, sometimes it is the smaller celebrations that can be the most charming.

St. Patrick's Day is celebrated by the Irish here, as it is everywhere else the Irish have settled. The difference is that the local version has a Mardi Gras touch, including floats. And whereas on Mardi Gras trinkets are thrown from the floats, the St. Patrick's revelers throw (what else?) food. You can bring home the makings of an Irish meal—cabbages, potatoes, carrots, and onions—if an Irish meal is your idea of a good time.

Two days later, the local Sicilians celebrate St. Joseph's Day by building altars to their patron saint. The altars are laden with food, from warm and savory vegetable dishes to cookies of every stripe. Many of these altars are built as repayment for favors granted to those who prayed to St. Joseph.

In another of this city's delightful entanglements, St. Joseph is also honored by the city's African-American community. By tradition, the Mardi Gras Indians—"tribes" of African-Americans who wear glittery native American costumes on Mardi Gras—make one appearance outside of the

These Mardi Gras costumes celebrate the great marriage of Louisiana's most favored hot sauce and its best-loved bivalve—the oyster.

Carnival parade. And that is on a weekend around St. Joseph's Day.

Only in New Orleans can you get over your hangover from an Irish party by cheering your way through a Sicilian parade while rocking to the rhythms of Africans dressed as Indians. It's as if the American melting pot went ahead and melted, right here in New Orleans. Believe me: New Orleanians wouldn't have it any other way.

The New Orleans Bar

A lively historical reflection on the city's "spiritual" life

by John DeMers

Thanks to its roots in the ever-imbibing Mediterranean world and its own much-proclaimed "Mardi Gras mentality," New Orleans and drinking have sounded natural in the same sentence as long as people have been talking about us. That, of course, is a very long time.

It follows that the city has made significant contributions to the history of the American cocktail—perhaps even the word *cocktail* itself. According to the preferred local legend (there are other, non–New Orleans theories, but none carries any more weight), it all goes back to Antoine Peychaud.

An oversized concoction known as the Hurricane, as created at Pat O'Brien's bar, dwarfs more reasonably-sized New Orleans libations.

If the man's name is now known primarily in association with Peychaud bitters, his fame strikes to the heart of America's history as a hard-drinking young nation. Peychaud, we're told, came to New Orleans from the Caribbean island of Santo Domingo in the late 1700s after a particularly violent slave uprising there. Many upper-crust planters made the crossing then, with the same save-their-skins idea in mind.

Once settled in the Crescent City, Peychaud took to dispensing a brandy-based cure-all from his apothecary on Royal Street. He eased a new word into the English language by serving this welcome relief in the larger side of a double-ended egg cup, known in French as a *coquetier*.

With this city's long-appreciated penchant for mispronunciation, *coquetier* quickly became *cock-tay* and then finally *cocktail*. According to the story, the idea of having a drink just because you felt like it spread from here to the rest of the still-young United States, and the New Orleans name *cocktail* went along with it.

Over the years, and into our own day, great New Orleans drinks remain the stuff of tourist excesses as well as local celebrations. Even with the evolution of public taste away from hard liquor and more toward white wine, it's hard to imagine New Orleans without Hurricanes, Sazeracs, Ramos Gin Fizzes, and a handful of other drinks either invented here or taken to a higher level so skillfully that they became "ours" nonetheless.

"When you go to New Orleans, my son," said a newspaper in the 1880s, "drink a Sazerac cocktail for me and one for yourself." Pride of place among local drinks is owned by this concoction of whiskey, sugar, bitters, and an anise-flavored cordial. The cocktail took its name from a French brandy put out by a company called Sazerac-du-Forge. The brandy was imported by John Schiller, who opened the Sazerac Coffee House in 1850 at No. 13 Exchange Alley.

When Thomas Handy took over the place in 1870, he adjusted the recipe to include just a dash of absinthe and a splash of red Peychaud bitters. Ironically, he replaced the brandy that had given the drink its name with American-made whiskey.

When the use of absinthe was banned in the United States in 1912, liqueurs like Ojen from Spain, Pernod from France, or Herbsaint from Louisiana were substituted to achieve the same touch of anise.

Today, the name *Sazerac* is diligently protected by the Sazerac Co., which actually licenses it to the Sazerac Bar at the Fairmont Hotel, which in turn served more than its share of the cocktails when it was the high-rolling Roosevelt.

The Hurricane (a newcomer compared with the Sazerac), made with passion-fruit flavoring, dark rum, and citrus juices, was created as a promotion at Pat O'Brien's Irish bar.

With the astronomical success of the Hurricane, the bar has even spun off a glass whose shape is recognizable anywhere—it is a footed glass, rounded at the bottom and tapering to a flared cylinder at the top. It is particularly well-known on Bourbon Street in the wee hours of the morning. Pat O's has given birth to other drinks bearing names like Cyclone, Squall, and Breeze.

Another historic favorite, the gin fizz (made of cream, gin, lemon juice, orange flower water, and egg whites) was created by Henry C. Ramos, a New Orleans bar owner who arrived in the city in 1888. At the time Ramos's Imperial Cabinet had a huge squad of bartenders, as many as thirty-five pouring out gin fizz after gin fizz during Carnival of 1915. The drink was a favorite of Louisiana governor Huey Long, who associated it with the bar at his beloved Roosevelt Hotel. When Long moved to Washington to serve in the U.S. Senate, he at first despaired of keeping the Ramos supply lines open. Eventually, the Kingfish imported his own bartender from New Orleans and made the drink, quite literally, the toast of the capital.

Along with the Sazerac, the Absinthe Suissesse and the Absinthe Frappe were the most famous New Orleans drinks associated with the namesake ingredient before its ban. Today, absinthe is typically replaced with Ojen.

A local variant on the Brandy Alexander that became a nationwide fad during Prohibition, Brandy Milk Punch, the primal version of the smoothie made of brandy, cream, sugar syrup, and egg, is great as a brunch aperitif. According to local lore, which invariably fights firewater with firewater, the Brandy Milk Punch helps cure hangovers.

We may not sip cool mint juleps on plantation verandahs, but on a hot New Orleans summer day there is nothing better than sitting on a French Quarter balcony, glass in hand, and watching the world go by.

A New Orleans Dine Around

Creole or Cajun, old or new, restaurants serve food and fantasy

by John DeMers

It is possible—even easy—to dine on history in New Orleans, both in terms of traditional recipes and in terms of restaurants still serving them in settings that exude history.

Nearly all of the city's oldest restaurants (in fact, the oldest one in America, Antoine's) are found in the French Quarter. This is where local European-recorded history began; this is where the settlement first became a city with aspirations of being the Paris of the New World.

There were a few eateries here before 1840, but **Antoine's** (713 St. Louis Street) is the oldest to survive into our modern day. It's unlikely that when Antoine Alciatore, then only twenty-seven, left Marseilles and opened a kind of no-frills boardinghouse on St. Louis Street, he could have foreseen what it would become.

Surely, he couldn't have foreseen the now famous dishes created at Antoine's, from oysters Rockefeller to pompano en papillote, or the presidents, movie stars, and authors who would dine within these walls. When Pope John Paul II visited New Orleans in 1988, it was Antoine's that cooked his meals.

Tujague's (823 Decatur Street) is by most accounts New Orleans' second-oldest restaurant—and it couldn't be more different from Antoine's. It reached legendary status under a certain Madame Begue, who dished up huge wine-kissed "second breakfasts" (a prototype of today's brunch) to merchants from the nearby French Market. Today, most of Tujague's traditions remain strong, thanks to the Latter family. Do not miss the shrimp rémoulade, boiled beef brisket with horseradish sauce, the hypergarlicked Chicken Bonne Femme, or the bread pudding.

Another of the older French Quarter eateries is **Galatoire's** (209 Bourbon Street), which made a home for itself on Bourbon Street in 1905, before any of that thoroughfare's current personality took hold.

If any restaurant here is more traditional than Antoine's, it would have to be Galatoire's, with its glittering dining room filled with high-society

Right: The lacy wrought-iron balconies of the French Quarter.
Opposite: *Henri Alciatore, maître d' in the Rex Room at Antoine's.*

Chef Emeril Lagasse, though originally from the East Coast, is a celebrity in his adopted city. He started at Commander's Palace and has since opened several successful restaurants of his own.

maine Wells and Archie Casbarian in the 1970s, Arnaud's today is as wonderful as anyone can remember it. The Shrimp Arnaud and Trout Meunière are musts here, and the bread pudding is the best.

Brennan's (417 Royal Street), while most famous for serving egg after egg after egg with too many cocktails at breakfast, is an insufficiently recognized gem for lunch or dinner. Many Creole classics were invented here, which makes Brennan's not only an interesting tourist spot but a part of history.

Commander's Palace (1403 Washington Avenue) in the Garden District remains a bridge between the Old World and the New, having reinvigorated traditional Creole cooking through the years with such well-known chefs de cuisine as Paul Prudhomme and Emeril Lagasse. With Jamie Shannon running the kitchen now, the Brennan family has every right to be confident that Commander's selection as a 1996 James Beard Award winner is no flash in the pan.

Near Commander's Palace, JoAnn Clevenger and chef Richard Benz keep creating wonderful things at the **Upperline** (1413 Upperline Street). In particular, Upperline is known for its "festival fetish," producing such events as a garlic festival, a duck festival, and festivals about whatever big event is in town.

A bit farther away from the maddening crowd, there's **Brigtsen's** (723 Dante Street), in the Riverbend section. Just past its tenth anniversary, Brigtsen's and its chef-owner, Frank Brigtsen, put one of the best spins going on creative Creole-Cajun flavors. Whatever Brigtsen is doing with rabbit, don't let it get away.

wave-and-wink, its veteran wait staff, and a menu taken from a Creole time capsule. What Galatoire's does, no one does better.

Arnaud's (813 Bienville Street) began operation in 1918 under the care of Arnaud Cazenave, a Frenchman so classy that before long he was known universally as "Count Arnaud." (He wasn't a count, in France or anywhere else—except maybe along Bienville Street!) With help from his daughter Ger-

Closer to downtown, the born-again Warehouse District has become a true restaurant row. Leading the renaissance has been **Emeril's** (800 Tchoupitoulas Street), established by former Brennan's chef Lagasse and reflecting his open-ended, highly personal style of cooking. If you sit at Emeril's food bar, you can even watch him cook.

Also in the Warehouse District (sometimes called the Arts District) you'll find **Mike's on the Avenue** (628 St. Charles Avenue), the restaurant that has done the most to convince locals that they can eat any cuisine on earth— all on the same plate, if they want to. Chef Mike Fennelly came to the city from New York by way of Santa Fe, and he offers the best of Thai-Southwestern-Mediterranean food. Mike's is chic, bright, airy, and deliciously unforgettable.

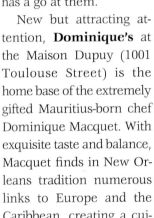

Lest you think a chef's departure is the worst thing in the world, you can walk around the corner and try the **Grill Room** at the Windsor Court (300 Gravier Street). Under Jeff Tunks's Asian-influenced hand, there's been no dramatic change of direction—it's just some of the world's best ingredients served in the city's most luxurious dining space.

Canal Street is New Orleans' own version of the Champs Élysées, and its single brightest spot has to be **Palace Cafe** (605 Canal Street), the Brennan family's loving (and expensive) reworking of the old Werlein's for Music building. It is graceful from its façade to its spiral staircase to its jazz-themed mural; and with veteran chef Robert Bruce in charge, the food has never been better.

At **Cafe Giovanni** (117 Decatur Street), just a few steps off Canal, local boy Duke LoCicero is turning Sicilian-influenced cooking on its ear. If you love Italian tastes and textures, you'll find most of them within these walls; and you just might envision them differently after LoCicero has a go at them.

New but attracting attention, **Dominique's** at the Maison Dupuy (1001 Toulouse Street) is the home base of the extremely gifted Mauritius-born chef Dominique Macquet. With exquisite taste and balance, Macquet finds in New Orleans tradition numerous links to Europe and the Caribbean, creating a cuisine as satisfying as it is unexpected.

Bella Luna (914 North Peters Street), overlooking the Mississippi River (with a very romantic view at night), is home to another young master of fusion cooking, Horst Pfeifer. Pfeifer filters his European birth and training through Southwestern cuisine to serve up Creole that tastes wonderful.

Chef Susan Spicer of **Bayona** (430 Dauphine Street) calls her style New World Cuisine, but she

Chef Paul Prudhomme, another of the city's celebrity chefs, has his own line of packaged seasonings. Here he samples the desserts at his own K-Paul's Louisiana Kitchen.

looks to the Old World for constant inspiration. Mediterranean flavors from Spain to Provence to Greece have a way of turning up in her food, though often outfitted for the journey by some technique picked up in Guatemala, India, or Singapore. Spicer's food has just about as many stamps as her passport.

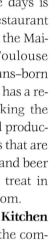

Right: The romantic dining room at Bella Luna overlooks the Mississippi River.
Opposite: You can eat Barbecued Oysters (recipe on page 134) and Crabmeat Shrimp Rolls while you watch the trolleys go by at Mike's on the Avenue.

Also riding high these days is Spicer's first great restaurant success, **The Bistro** at the Maison de Ville (727 Toulouse Street). The New Orleans–born chef here, Greg Picolo, has a remarkable flair for picking the best of things local and producing wonderful versions that are all his own. The wine and beer list is an extra-special treat in this intimate dining room.

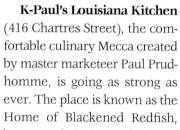

K-Paul's Louisiana Kitchen (416 Chartres Street), the comfortable culinary Mecca created by master marketeer Paul Prudhomme, is going as strong as ever. The place is known as the Home of Blackened Redfish, but apart from its catchy innovations K-Paul's serves up some of the finest, most authentic country cooking in this or any other city.

Over on the other side of the French Quarter is **Peristyle** (1041 Dumaine Street), a quirky place first made famous by the late chef John Neal. Peristyle is now the province of Anne Kearny—and a creative, satisfying province it is. If you want to go somewhere your friends haven't been, check out Peristyle—it won't disappoint.

Leaving behind the recognized tourist districts (but right on the way to the expanded New Orleans Museum of Art), **Gabrielle** (3201 Esplanade Avenue), keeps competing for world-class honors. Chef-owners Greg and Mary Sonnier pick up their share of dining awards, but the truly honored are all those who make it inside for a memorable Cajun-Creole meal.

On your way in or out of New Orleans you can see how in recent years fine dining has spread all over the place. In suburban Metairie, **Andrea's** (3100 Nineteenth Street, Metairie) dishes up some of the best regional Italian food this side of Capri (which chef-owner Andrea Apuzzo happens to call home).

On the fast-growing north shore of Lake Pontchartrain, check out **La Provence** (US 190, Lacombe) and say hi to white-haired chef-gentleman-poet Chris Kerageorgiou.

Finally, don't miss the **Abita Brewpub** (72011 Holly Street, Abita Springs), an offshoot of a highly successful microbrewery. After all, the very best thing we know to do with cool, fresh spring water is turn it into cold, fresh beer.

Part Two: The New Orleans Kitchen

Outfitting the home cook for the pursuit of pleasure

by Marcelle Bienvenu

Visit a New Orleans kitchen, the very heart and soul of the cuisine, and you will watch in amazement as the cook performs magic, waving a skilled seasoning hand over a simmering pot, giving a stir to another, and plucking a roasting pan out of a hot oven—all in one graceful turn around his or her domain.

New Orleans cooks are all well tutored in the art of "making do," that is, using what is at hand. Each kitchen is an efficient one. Nothing goes to waste. Chicken or duck carcasses, or beef bones, are simmered long and slow to make stock and broth for gumbos, soups, or stews. The residuals of yesterday's roasted chicken may well become today's chicken salad. Whatever the hunter or fisherman brings home may be broiled, boiled, fried, smoked, grilled, or otherwise prepared for the table.

Garden vegetables and fruits, if not consumed fresh, are canned, pickled, or frozen for later. Day-old bread is made into *pain perdu* (lost bread) or creamy, smooth bread pudding. There is a saying that the people can get along with very little and some-

times with a heck of a lot less. For example, when there's not much more than a handful of leftover cooked rice; the New Orleans cook can add a little milk, a sprinkling of sugar and cinnamon, perhaps a splash of vanilla—and *voilà,* he or she has calas, a tasty rice cake, or perhaps a delightful rice pudding. Keep in mind that there are no hard-and-fast rules about the cuisine. As with jazz, you can improvise. Add a note (or a pinch of spice) here, hold a sound longer (simmer it just a bit more) there. There are as many recipes for gumbo as there are bayous and waterways that crisscross the state. This is a cuisine of ad lib.

Because of this delightful impromptu quality, Creole and Cajun cooking have long resisted generalization. In the 1980s, when Louisiana cuisine became a national phenomenon, so much of what was said or written was just plain wrong.

For instance, neither Creole nor Cajun cuisine is noted for being hot and spicy. Yes, of course, we like our foods well flavored. And yes, of course, Tabasco sauce does hail from Avery Island, just south of New Iberia, which is just south of Lafayette, Louisiana. But no legitimate Louisiana cook would answer the question "What's your food like?" by saying, "Well, it's real hot." Forget what

Opposite: In the old-fashioned kitchen at Houmas House, cooking implements from colonial times hang over the fireplace. **Bottom, left:** Copper skimmers and ladles. **Above:** Copper pots.

you may have encountered in that Cajun eatery in Juneau or Jakarta.

What any real Louisiana cook embraces is flavor—with the attitude that more is better. Flavor and heat are not the same thing, so many Creole and Cajun classics are not hot or spicy at all.

In what must qualify as the ultimate ridiculous commentary, tourists have been known to complain in some of our finest restaurants that the food just isn't spicy enough. One supposes that, short of slapping these folks around, a suggestion of Tabasco is the only way to fly.

This "more flavor" approach is realized in Creole and Cajun cooking in a number of ways, most of which add up to a complex layering of seasonings. The basis of most dishes is onion, bell pepper, and celery, chopped and sautéed at the start of so many recipes that it's known (in ever-Catholic south Louisiana) as the Holy Trinity. Garlic is always close at hand and liberally used, as befits a cuisine with overtones borrowed from France, Spain, and Sicily.

And then there is the matter of the roux, that flavoring, coloring, and thickening agent used in Louisiana dish after Louisiana dish. Any trained French chef would recognize the word: an equal combination of fat and flour that is continually stirred while cooking in a heavy pan on the stovetop and results in a very useful culinary paste. But he or she probably wouldn't recognize roux as perfected over generations in south Louisiana. Ranging from amber to nearly black, it is used in everything from gumbo to étouffée to

*Below: A heavy bottomed cast-iron skillet is best for making a roux. **Right:** No good New Orleans kitchen is without heavy cast-iron pots.*

sauce for meat or seafood. Roux is as much a part of Louisiana cooking as the Holy Trinity.

And finally, trying to speak broadly, there is the manner of cooking. Those fine Creole palaces devoted to hollandaise-sauced dishes notwithstanding, most Louisiana dishes are prepared in a single pot, usually slow-cooked to grab the most flavor and tenderness from the least expensive ingredients. Jambalaya, our version of Spanish paella, certainly qualifies, as does étouffée (the name translates as "smothered," referring to the cooking method). And so does gumbo, that delicious and immeasurably versatile Afro-Creole born-again version of French bouillabaisse.

Despite our being in the last decade of the twentieth century, the basic implements found in a typical New Orleans kitchen are still few and simple. Nary a kitchen is without a collection of satiny-smooth, **black cast-iron pots and pans.** They cook evenly and hold heat better than any other type of cookware, thus making them ideal for the kind of dishes prepared here. The larger ones are for simmering gumbos, stews, and a variety of meats and poultry.

Large **skillets** are ideal for cooking corn breads and pan-frying a great variety of fresh fish available from the waterways, adjoining bays, and the Gulf of Mexico. Smaller skillets are used for sautéing the inevitable combination of hand-chopped onions, bell peppers, celery, and sometimes garlic.

These black iron pots are used so often, someone once said that if you're ever in a pinch, simply pour some water in one and it could create a gumbo on its own. They are held so sacred that they are often passed down from one generation to the next. My father's collection was included in his will and dispensed to his children according to his wishes.

Long-simmered stocks and sauces are made in a variety of **stockpots** and **saucepans**. Because of the affinity for fried seafoods, large, **deep frying pots** or an **electric deep-fryer** is always handy.

The tradition of making homemade sausages is still alive and well, making a **hand-operated meat grinder** or an **electric grinder,** both with several plates or dies, a given in most kitchens. Here, the option is usually for the hand-operated type, simply because it's much easier to stuff the casings by hand through a funnel.

In our subtropical climate, there's a lot of smoking, grilling, and barbecuing going on. A small **smoker** (an enclosed container or pit in which foods can slowly mingle with smoke) that doubles as a grill or barbecue is usually found on the patio or in the backyard. Everything from meats and poultry to shrimp and fish may end up on this well-used implement.

The same goes for large **boiling pots** set atop butane burners. Incredible amounts of crabs, shrimp, and crawfish are cooked in fragrant, spicy water on just about any given weekend during the warmer months.

Since rice is served practically daily, an **electric rice cooker** has found its way into modern kitchens, although the old-timers can steam a batch of rice in just about any pot available.

Black, white-speckled **granite roasters** come in handy for roasting chicken, beef, pork, and wild game. (Louisiana is called a sportsman's paradise because of the wild ducks, geese, rabbits, and deer that are abundant here.)

Spices and dried herbs are stored in large (not small, because seasonings are used in healthy but discerning doses here) widemouthed jars.

Bunches of bay leaves, ropes of locally grown garlic, and strings of Tabasco or cayenne peppers hang from hooks in the dry pantry. Fresh herbs such as thyme, parsley, and shallots (called green onions locally) are found in many kitchen gardens, as is mint with which to flavor mint juleps, lemonade, and iced tea.

And always, right alongside the large **chopping board,** are a few finely honed knives with which to chop, mince, debone, or fillet. Cooking utensils, such as several sizes of **wooden spoons** and large **stainless-steel spoons, spatulas,** and **ladles,** are the only other items you need to assemble New Orleans dishes.

New Orleanians take food as seriously as they take anything on earth. It is said that the people have a twenty-four-hour-a-day love affair with food. Meals are regarded by all as potential sources of pleasure, not merely as sustenance. Table talk not only includes what was eaten at your last meal, the hopes and expectations for this meal, but first and foremost, where and what you will eat tomorrow. Be assured, it will be good!

Top: This old-fashioned rotisserie was used to roast meat over a fireplace.
Bottom, left: *Wooden spoons and a spatula.*
Below: *An antique buttermilk churn.*

New Orleans Ingredients

A few notes on the usual and unusual products in every well-stocked New Orleans kitchen

Andouille sausage

Artichoke

Basil

ANDOUILLE: Called by the name it often carries in France, this is south Louisiana's smoked sausage extraordinaire. Traditionally, it's made of pork—a by-product of the autumn or winter *boucherie,* the rural get-together focusing on slaughtering a hog. Today, only a few residents make their own. The taste is peppery, but the smoked flavor is more important to most New Orleans recipes than any amount of spice. If you can't get andouille, use another spicy sausage, though the flavor will be different.

ARTICHOKES: The local Sicilian population can claim credit for teaching New Orleanians to love these vegetables. The base or heart is favored in casseroles, though the most common rendition involves "stuffing" the whole artichoke between its leaves with an Italianate bread-crumb mixture. Oyster and artichoke soup is a delicious New Orleans classic.

BASIL: Basil found a market with voodoo queen Marie Laveau and her many fearful followers, who grew it in their front yards to ward off the evil eye. All mysticism aside, New Orleans cooks love what fresh basil does for a dish—especially one with tomatoes.

BAY LEAVES: The dried leaves of the laurel tree are a recurring ingredient in Creole and Cajun cooking. This leaf never truly cooks down, making it inedible, and is virtually the only favored flavoring that has to be removed from the dish before serving. But the taste it supplies during slow cooking earns it a place of respect indeed.

BELL PEPPERS: Also known as capsicums, and as sweet peppers—presumably to set them apart from hot peppers. They are traditionally used green, chopped with onion and celery, and sautéed as seasoning for Creole dishes. In New Creole cooking, yellow and red versions are used to add color—a concern that possibly never crossed the minds of most New Orleans cooks of the past.

BLACK-EYED PEAS: A taste acquired from the countryside far beyond the New Orleans city limits, black-eyed peas are small and extremely flavorful. Named for their telltale black dot, black-eyes are terrific stewed with salty meat just like red beans, cooked more simply as a vegetable side dish, or cooked and then marinated in vinaigrette as a delicious Deep South salad.

BLUE CRAB: These are sold with either hard or soft shells, in a variety of sizes. Though we hear much about Chesapeake Bay crabs,

Louisiana is the primary shipper of live male crabs to the Atlantic Coast markets, with lesser amounts of mature female crabs shipped to Hawaii. The state's soft-shell crabs tend to draw a higher price than those from any other state. Backfin or jumbo lump meat is the most expensive among four types of picked meat: it comes in the largest clumps and includes the fewest shell fragments. Soft-shell blue crab sandwiches are a New Orleans specialty that you can purchase to eat as you stroll.

BOUDIN: Borrowed directly from Louisiana's French ancestors, boudin is a type of country sausage made year-round, but particularly around the time of the *boucherie,* the hog butchering. For the record, there are two popular boudins in Louisiana: white, made with a stuffing of rice, and black, made with blood from the hog. The latter is sometimes referred to as blood sausage, as it is in the Old World.

CAYENNE PEPPER: This is the powder in the jar that's increasingly sold as ground red pepper but is still called by its old name, cayenne. It supplies much of the mouthburn in Creole and Cajun cooking, most often in concert with black and white pepper. It is also a notable ingredient in the omnipresent Creole and Cajun seasoning mixes.

CELERY: Along with onion and bell pepper, celery is part of the Holy Trinity of seasonings used in dish upon dish. Nearly always the bright green stalks are finely chopped, mixed with the other two vegetables (also chopped), and sautéed. If you walk through an old-time

Louisiana town near suppertime, you'll go nuts from this mixture's wonderful smell.

COCKTAIL SAUCE: At seafood boils around New Orleans, gallons of this sauce are imbibed with shrimp, crawfish, and especially raw oysters on the half shell. Zealots of course insist on mixing their own, but it's always a catsup base with plenty of pungent horseradish, some brand of hot pepper sauce, and a squeeze or two of lemon.

CRAWFISH: There was a time when northerners pronounced it "crayfish" just to make Creoles and Cajuns mad, and they tirelessly mocked the entire notion that these tiny "mudbugs" were edible. The French have always known better. And finally, so does just about everyone else. In fact, tons of crawfish each year stream off to places like New York and Paris. Generally, only the tails are used in cooking (despite constant exhortations to "suck the heads"). These tails can be purchased fresh or frozen in bags surrounded by their own "fat." When you use crawfish, don't wash off the "fat"; it holds the best of the crawfish's flavor. In recent years, Louisiana crawfish have been competing with imports raised in China. Needless to say, such treason is not tolerated around the Atchafalaya Basin, where the world's best crawfish are harvested.

CREOLE MUSTARD: A distinct departure from the smooth traditions of Dijon and especially from the bland yellow ballpark preparation known across America, Creole mustard, with its coarsely ground seeds, is as pungent as it

Bay leaves (fresh)

Bell peppers

Boudin

Crawfish

Eggplant

Garlic

Hot peppers

Okra

is grainy. It has the sinus-clearing punch that's normally associated with horseradish, and is the basis of several sauces—including rémoulade for shrimp. It's also terrific on a ham sandwich. Historically, this Creole mustard has been made by steeping the seeds in vinegar. German immigrants brought the mustard seeds from Austria and Holland.

CREOLE SEASONING: Here's a shortcut home cooks can learn from professional chefs: mix your seasonings in advance. Better still, find a mix you really love and buy it. Salt is the predominant flavor in almost all the mixes—for such is the local taste. But there's always ground pepper—black, white, and red—garlic powder (a lot!), and other spices. This being Louisiana, some mixes are sold as Creole and some as Cajun. Don't try to find any difference.

EGGPLANT: The use of eggplant, or aubergine, in New Orleans cooking was picked up from the Sicilians, who picked it up from the Greeks, who picked it up from the Turks. Every home cook has his or her favorite seafood stuffing for eggplant.

FILÉ: This is a powder made by grinding dried sassafras leaves. It's an old Choctaw Indian ingredient, picked up by the European settlers around New Orleans and still used as a thickener in gumbo. You'll see "filé gumbo" on some menus around town, which almost certainly means that no okra was used to thicken it during cooking. And you'll hear of it in Hank Williams's famous refrain "Jambalaya, crawfish pie, filé gumbo!"

FLOUNDER: A beloved New Orleans fish, flounder is often served stuffed, though it is great simply broiled with a light sprinkle of pepper, too. Flounder has the leanest, driest flesh of any fish caught in Louisiana—and the absence of moisture makes it perfect for freezing. There are, the experts say, few ice crystals to cut the flesh and turn it to mush. So it can be enjoyed anytime, anywhere.

GREENS: Turnip and mustard greens are the most popular greens in New Orleans. Greens are poor folks' food, to be sure. Yet, when they are steamed or smothered, then served up (as in "a mess of greens") with a sprinkle or three of peppered vinegar, they seem like a pleasure to measure against beluga caviar.

GRITS: This quintessentially Southern food, also known as hominy grits, is a white, mild-tasting starch made by coarsely grinding the hulled kernels of mature dried corn to produce a substance that is similar to cornmeal. Grits is usually boiled and served as an accompaniment to eggs and sausage at breakfast or with fish. Authentic grits is served with a pat of butter on top.

GROUPER: Yellow edge, also called yellowfin, grouper is the most common type landed in Louisiana, followed by the huge Warsaw and the Snowy. As anyone who has tasted it will avow, the meat of grouper is white, lean, and flaky, perfect for just about any style of cooking. The "gourmet grouper," however, is known as the scamp. It is caught only in small quantities.

HOT SAUCE: For Louisiana food fetishists seeking searing flavor, a number of old families have just the thing. Led by the McIlhenny family of Avery Island (producers of world-famous Tabasco sauce) all these entrepreneurs take some version of jalapeño or habanero peppers, reduce them to a fiery mash, then extend them into a sauce with vinegar and other liquids.

MIRLITON: This is the squashlike fruit also called vegetable pear, christophene, or chayote. Widely grown in the Caribbean and Latin America, it is especially beloved in Louisiana. Mirlitons are generally stuffed and baked in the same way as eggplant and green bell peppers.

OKRA: Also known as ladies' fingers, this vegetable is a bit of an oddity unless you're from the Deep South, where it's used as a thickener in gumbo by the Creoles and Cajuns and is pickled or fried by just about everyone else. Okra has a long history: it was cultivated by the ancient Sumerians and used extensively by the Egyptians (who pounded it to make papyrus). A favorite of African jungle tribes, it reached America with the slaves along with its original name in Tshi—*gombo.* Since the slaves were kept naked during their voyages to bondage, it is said they preserved the gombo seeds just about the only way they could, by hiding them in their ears.

OYSTERS: These bivalves have been cultivated for at least two thousand years, their name deriving from ancient Greek. Many of the world's coastal regions produce oysters of one kind or another, but the ones grown in Louisiana are among the juiciest and briniest anywhere. Most are devoured in their natural state, chilled just a bit to make them more refreshing and dipped lightly in cocktail sauce. The remaining oysters turn up in an infinite number of Creole preparations.

PARSLEY: Though many cuisines embrace cilantro as their cooling green sprinkle of choice, New Orleanians are traditional enough to still like a sprig of parsley as garnish or minced for extra flavor.

Parsley

PECAN: With the occasional politician excepted, the pecan is the official nut of Louisiana. It's grown here, it's sweet and crunchy, it's wonderful. It is used mostly in sweets (from pralines to pecan pie) but also turns up on fish and vegetables. Walnuts make reasonable substitutes—just don't tell New Orleanians you think so.

Pecans

POMPANO: Mark Twain called the pompano "delicious as the less criminal forms of sin." The locals sometimes call it sole, placing it squarely in the league of another world-class fish. And most chefs place it far ahead of any sole except Dover. Though pompano range from Massachusetts to Brazil, more are consumed in the United States than anywhere else on the globe. Virtually every famous Creole restaurant has its own special preparation, from the famous pompano en papillote to the simple sautéed fillet covered with crabmeat.

Red beans

RED BEANS: Simply put, these are just red kidney beans. Yet, drawing inspiration from the

Rosemary

Scallions

Seafood boil

Shrimp

Squash

Spanish Caribbean, New Orleans came up with the notion of slow-cooking beans with salty meat and seasonings, then ladling them over white rice. On Mondays, most restaurants in New Orleans offer red beans as specials—a practice that hearkens back to the time when Mama did the laundry on Monday and put red beans on to cook while the wash went on and on.

REDFISH: Touch the black spot near the tail of a redfish and you are touching a legend. According to one story, the redfish was what Christ used to feed the multitude, and that spot was where his thumb touched. Even without the religious significance, this member of the croaker and rum family finds a special place in Creole cuisine. Redfish courtbouillon is a big, satisfying stew, while redfish chambord presents this seafood's sophisticated side—poached, then topped with diced artichokes, mushrooms, and a glaze. Cajun blackened redfish is now served all over the world. As a result, Louisiana's redfish supply was almost wiped out some years back, forcing the state and even the federal government to protect this glorious taste for the future. The closely related black drum fish, and also tuna, can be used as substitutes.

RICE: You'd have to go to China to find a population that eats as much rice per capita as Louisiana does. That's because in field after field across south Louisiana, long-grain rice is the staple crop. In fact, several Asian nations have purchased Louisiana rice over the years.

Innumerable dishes are served with steamed white rice, a list led by New Orleans red beans and rice, not to mention jambalaya and dirty rice, in which ingredients are added before the rice is steamed.

ROSEMARY: New Orleans follows the French lead in pairing this herb most commonly with lamb, but local cooks also know how much its unique pungency can add to a sauce or robust meat stew.

SCALLIONS: These long green onions, also known as spring onions, tend to be mistakenly called shallots by New Orleans cooks, perhaps a mere mangling of scallions—which is their correct name. The green tops give special texture and flavor to gumbos and stews.

SEAFOOD BOIL: A commercial spice blend used to flavor the liquid in which seafood is to be cooked. It usually contains mustard seeds, peppercorns, bay leaves, allspice, cloves, ginger, and hot pepper. Though still known around New Orleans as crab boil, the flavor is most often experienced these days in boiled shrimp or crawfish.

SHALLOTS: Few words are misused more often in New Orleans' food vocabulary. Over the years, *shallots* has referred primarily to green onions or scallions. For our purposes, scallions are called precisely that, with *shallots* reserved for the small, white and purple French onion.

SHARK: At least nine varieties of shark are listed as fished in Louisiana waters, being found along the entire coast but mostly out of

Grand Isle and Venice. Most esteemed culinarily is the mako, quite close to swordfish in taste and texture, followed at a distance by bull, Atlantic sharpnose, and silky. Shark meat is very white, lean, and versatile in cooking. As shark is cartilaginous, it is also boneless.

SHRIMP: This is America's favorite seafood, with a distinctive taste and tender, juicy meat. Shrimp, called prawns in much of the world, is one of the Creole cook's favorite ingredients—a fact proven by the immense variety of Creole dishes that require it. The Gulf of Mexico and the brackish waters at the mouth of the Mississippi River are the country's most important shrimping grounds, with a season from May through December.

SPECKLED TROUT: Known more officially as the spotted sea trout, this is the "speck," historically the top-selling commercial fish in Louisiana's saltwater marshes. Terrific to catch and terrific to eat, this one, too, has been the subject of survival concerns in recent years. The supply seems to be doing better.

SQUASH: Native Americans grew squash in the vicinity of New Orleans long before the Europeans arrived. Varieties such as summer squash and yellow crookneck squash are grown on small farms that surround the city.

TASSO: This Cajun country pork product is almost never eaten on its own but is used as a seasoning meat. It lends its smokiness and saltiness to beans and soups—even, these days, to crawfish dishes and sophisticated cream sauces for pastas.

THYME: Like its popular cohort basil, thyme is an ancient European herb with a pedigree in medicine as well as in flavoring. Cooks in New Orleans use thyme liberally (both dried and fresh) in soups, stews, and sauces.

WHITE SHRIMP: These are sometimes known as white prawns, or recently as Gulf prawns. Though not prawns in the technical sense, they are the premium large shrimp of Louisiana and almost always draw the highest price at market. They are tender, easy to peel, and do not have the slight iodine flavor sometimes associated with other shrimp.

YAMS: It was growers in the state of Louisiana who decided to call the sweet potatoes they grew *yams* and there has been endless confusion on the topic ever since. The Louisiana yam is a moist-fleshed, bright orange-yellow sweet potato that's terrific when cooked with butter and brown sugar.

YELLOWFIN TUNA: This fish was not caught here at all until 1980 but now is a major crop. The best yellowfin is eaten raw as sashimi in Japanese restaurants. But all yellowfin is excellent, particularly when marinated and grilled. Less expensive, but similar in quality, are the bluefin and blackfin, also caught in Louisiana waters.

ZUCCHINI: The popularity of zucchini, or courgette, in New Orleans comes via the Sicilian immigration, since Sicilians join Greeks in relishing these long, rich, dark green squashes. Generally speaking, the smallest and youngest zucchini are the best.

Tasso

Thyme

Yams

Zucchini

Part Three: The Recipes

Basic recipes for seasonings, stocks, and sauces

SEASONINGS

Roux

Used to be, young Creole and Cajun cooks were introduced to their art with the words "First you make a roux." Increasingly, this thickening and flavoring mix of flour and oil (some cooks prefer butter) is used sparingly at the end of the cooking process, affording the cook a greater degree of control.

1 cup (250 ml) vegetable oil
1 cup (110 g) all-purpose (plain) flour

Place the oil in a large, heavy-bottomed skillet over medium heat. Whisk the flour into the oil and cook slowly, watching carefully and stirring constantly until the roux reaches the desired color, about 10 to 12 minutes for a light, tan-colored roux; about 15 to 18 minutes for a medium-dark roux; and about 20 to 25 minutes for deep, dark brown roux. If the roux burns, discard it and start over. A scorched roux will contribute a bitter flavor to the finished dish. If you are using the roux to thicken a gumbo or sauce, stir about ½ cup (125 ml) liquid from the main dish into it to stop it from cooking. Once it's premixed in this way, it is less likely to form lumps when it's added to the main dish. Yields 1 cup.

Time Estimates

Time estimates are for preparation only (excluding cooking) and are based on the assumption that a food processor or blender will be used.

  ⏲ *quick and very easy to prepare*

  ⏲⏲ *relatively easy; 15 to 30 minutes' preparation*

  ⏲⏲⏲ *takes more than 30 minutes to prepare*

Seafood Boil

8 whole allspice berries
1 hot red chile pepper
1 tablespoon Creole seasoning
1 garlic clove, crushed
1 bay leaf
10 black peppercorns

Add all ingredients to boiling water. Let boil for about 1 minute to release the flavors before adding the seafood. Yields enough flavoring for 4 lb (2 kg) of seafood.

STOCKS AND SAUCES

Creole Sauce

4 tablespoons butter
½ cup (90 g) chopped green bell pepper
    (capsicum)
½ cup (90 g) chopped red bell pepper
    (capsicum)
½ cup (90 g) chopped onion
2 cups (510 g) diced tomatoes
½ teaspoon dried tarragon
½ teaspoon dried oregano
½ teaspoon dried basil
½ teaspoon dried thyme
1 tablespoon Creole seasoning
2 garlic cloves, minced
1 teaspoon Tabasco sauce
Salt and black pepper

Melt the butter in a large sauté pan over medium heat. Add the remaining ingredients and sauté for 1 to 2 minutes. Simmer to reduce the liquid to one-third its volume, cool. Yields about 1 cup (250 ml).

Béarnaise Sauce

4 egg yolks at room temperature, beaten well
Juice of 1 lemon (3 tablespoons)
2 tablespoons white wine, preferably Chablis
    or dry vermouth
1 teaspoon finely crumbled dried tarragon
1 cup (2 sticks, or 225 g) butter, melted
Salt and black pepper

In the top of a double boiler, beat the egg yolks, lemon juice, wine, and tarragon with a whisk until the mixture thickens, 3 to 5 minutes. Remove from heat. In a slow, steady stream, add the melted butter. Continue whisking until all the butter has been incorporated into a smooth, fluffy sauce. Season with salt and pepper. Yields about 1½ cups (375 ml).

Hollandaise Sauce

6 egg yolks, beaten well
1¼ cups (2½ sticks, or 290 g) butter, melted
Salt, white pepper, and ground red pepper
    (cayenne)
1 tablespoon fresh lemon juice

In the top of a double boiler, combine the egg yolks and 1½ tablespoons water. Beat with a wire whisk over hot, but not boiling, water. Slowly add the butter and whip until the sauce begins to thicken. Add the salt and white and red pepper. Then whisk in the lemon juice. Yields about 2 cups (500 ml).

Fish Stock

1 lb (450 g) fish bones, cleaned
½ cup (100 g) chopped shallots
½ leek, chopped
½ cup (60 g) chopped celery
½ cup (8 g) chopped fresh parsley
1 pinch dried thyme
1 bay leaf
3 black peppercorns
½ cup (125 ml) white wine

Place 3 quarts (liters) of water in a stockpot, add all ingredients, and bring to a boil. Reduce the heat and simmer for 15 minutes. Remove from the heat, skim, and strain through a strainer. Either use immediately or refrigerate until ready to use. The stock can be kept refrigerated up to 3 days. Yields about 2½ quarts (liters).

Chicken Stock

2 lb (1 kg) chicken bones
1 cup (110 g) chopped carrots
½ cup (90 g) chopped onion

½ cup (60 g) chopped celery with leaves
½ cup (8 g) chopped fresh parsley
Pinch of whole thyme
1 bay leaf

Bring 8 quarts (liters) of water to a boil in a large stockpot and add all the ingredients. Simmer for 1 hour, until the liquid is reduced by half. Allow the stock to cool, skim off all fat that gathers at the surface, and refrigerate until ready to use—up to 3 days. Yields about 4 quarts (liters).

Beef Stock

2 lb (1 kg) beef bones
2⅔ cups (450 g) roughly chopped onions
2 cups (225 g) sliced carrots
1 cup (170 g) chopped leeks
1⅓ cups (140 g) chopped celery with leaves
1 cup (15 g) chopped fresh parsley
1 teaspoon dried thyme
2 bay leaves
½ head garlic, peeled
½ cup (130 g) tomato paste
5 black peppercorns

Preheat the oven to 450°F (230°C, gas mark 8), and roast the bones until brown, about 30 minutes. Place them in a stockpot with 8 quarts (liters) of water, add all remaining ingredients, and bring to a boil. Reduce heat and simmer for 2 to 3 hours, skimming as needed. Strain the stock through a strainer, return it to the pot, and boil to reduce it to one-third its volume. This stock can be kept in the refrigerator for 3 to 4 days. Yields about 4 quarts (liters).

Fish Velouté

¾ cup (90 g) all-purpose (plain) flour
¼ cup (½ stick, or 60 g) butter
3 cups (750 ml) Fish Stock (page 40), hot
½ cup (125 ml) heavy (whipping) cream
Salt and white pepper to taste
Nutmeg to taste

In a medium-sized saucepan over medium heat, make a roux with the flour and butter and stir until it is light brown, 10 to 12 minutes. Add the hot fish stock and boil until the reduced liquid coats a spoon. Add the cream and boil for 5 minutes, then season to taste with salt, white pepper, and nutmeg. Strain through a strainer. Yields about 2 cups (500 ml).

Marchand de Vin Sauce

3 tablespoons butter
3 tablespoons all-purpose (plain) flour
½ cup (90 g) minced onion
½ cup (35 g) finely chopped fresh mushrooms
1 tomato, peeled, seeded, and minced
1 clove garlic, minced
1 celery rib, minced
2 tablespoons minced fresh parsley
2 bay leaves
¼ teaspoon dried thyme
1 cup (250 ml) red wine
1 cup (250 ml) Beef Stock (this page)
Salt and black pepper

In a saucepan, combine the butter and flour together to make a roux. Cook until the roux begins to darken, then stir in the onion and mushrooms. Add the remaining ingredients and simmer for 45 minutes. Keep the sauce warm. Yields about 2 cups (500 ml).

PAIN PERDU AND BEIGNETS

PAIN PERDU

I love the name of this dessert or brunch item—lost bread. The old Creoles took special delight in devising new life for foods that had passed their prime, and since fresh French bread was always available, day-old French bread was always being displaced. Like bread pudding, here's a great example of "recycling" before it was chic. And yes, Pain Perdu is another version of French toast. ☉

Pain Perdu (left) and Beignets (right).

2 eggs, beaten
1 cup (250 ml) milk
1 tablespoon granulated sugar
1 pinch salt
$\frac{1}{4}$ teaspoon vanilla extract
6 slices day-old French bread
2 tablespoons butter
1 tablespoon vegetable oil
$\frac{1}{2}$ teaspoon cinnamon
Powdered sugar or cane (golden) syrup

Thoroughly combine the eggs, milk, sugar, salt, and vanilla in a bowl. Soak the slices of day-old French bread in this mixture for 2 to 3 minutes. In a large heavy skillet, heat the butter and oil, add the bread slices one or two slices at a time, and fry until they are golden brown on both sides. Sprinkle with cinnamon and serve hot with either powdered sugar or cane syrup. Serves 3 to 6.

BEIGNETS ☉☉☉

1 cup (250 ml) scalded milk
1 egg, beaten
2 tablespoons vegetable oil
2 tablespoons granulated sugar
1 envelope (7 g) dry yeast
3 cups (340 g) all-purpose (plain) flour
1 teaspoon salt
$\frac{1}{2}$ teaspoon ground cinnamon
$\frac{1}{2}$ teaspoon ground nutmeg
Vegetable oil for deep-frying
Powdered sugar

In a large bowl, combine the milk and egg with the 2 tablespoons vegetable oil and the sugar. Blend thoroughly, then add the dry yeast and stir to dissolve. Sift together the flour, salt, and spices, then add half to the yeast mixture. Mix well. Add the remaining flour and knead to incorporate it. Form a large ball, cover, and let double in bulk, about 40 minutes. Punch down and knead until dough is elastic.

On a floured board, roll out the dough to a thickness of $\frac{1}{4}$ in ($\frac{1}{2}$ cm) and cut into 24 5-in (13-cm) squares. Cover, allow to rise again, about 45 minutes.

Pour 3 in (8 cm) of oil into a deep-fryer or tall, heavy-bottomed saucepan, heat to 375°F (190°C). Drop in the dough squares a few at a time, cooking and turning them until golden. Remove with a slotted spoon and drain on absorbent paper. Dust with powdered sugar. Serve hot, 3 to an order. Serves 8.

EGGS HUSSARDE & EGGS SARDOU

Brennan's

EGGS HUSSARDE

The origin of this dish is mysterious. It may simply have been named for a friend of the Brennan family—no one seems to remember—or it may hark back to the French word *hussard* for soldier. ☯☯☯

1 cup (250 ml) Hollandaise Sauce (page 40)
1 cup (250 ml) Marchand de Vin Sauce
  (page 41)
8 large thin slices of cooked ham
8 slices tomato, cut ¼-in (½-cm) thick
2 teaspoons olive oil
8 eggs
8 Holland rusks or toasted English muffin
  halves
Paprika

Eggs Sardou, another brunch favorite.

Preheat the broiler (grill). Warm the hollandaise sauce in the top of a double boiler set over simmering water. Warm the marchand de vin sauce in a separate pot over low heat or in a microwave. Keep warm.

Broil the ham until browned on both sides, about 4 minutes per side. Remove and keep warm. Place the tomato slices on the broiling (grill) pan, brush with the oil, and broil (grill) until heated through and lightly browned on top, about 3 minutes. Set aside and keep warm.

Working with no more than 4 eggs at a time, slide the eggs into barely simmering water and poach for 3 to 5 minutes, until the yolk is set (for softer eggs, poach for 3 minutes; for harder eggs, continue for 5 minutes). Lift out of the water with a slotted spoon. Repeat with the remaining 4 eggs.

To assemble the dish, place a slice of the ham across each Holland rusk or English muffin. Cover with the marchand de vin sauce, followed by a slice of tomato, and then a poached egg. Spoon hollandaise sauce over the top, and add color with a sprinkle of paprika. Serves 4.

EGGS SARDOU

This elaborate egg dish, one of several that are popular at brunch in New Orleans, is named after Victorien Sardou—the French playwright famous for his melodramas, including the one that inspired the heavy-breathing Puccini opera *Tosca*. Sardou had breakfast at Antoine's in 1908. ☯☯☯

4¾ cups (1¼ liters) creamed spinach
12 fresh medium-sized artichoke bottoms,
  boiled
12 poached eggs
3 cups (750 ml) Hollandaise Sauce
  (page 40), warm
Paprika

Spoon the hot creamed spinach into the centers of 6 dinner plates. Arrange 2 hot artichoke bottoms on top of the spinach. Place a hot poached egg on each artichoke bottom and cover with hot hollandaise sauce. Sprinkle with paprika. Serves 6.

GRILLADES & GRITS

Brennan's

GRILLADES

For dinner, breakfast, brunch, or any other time, here's a local favorite that's sure to satisfy. The word *grillades* (pronounced gree-yads) refers to the meat, naturally, though in most good renditions the hearty reddish brown sauce is the real star. ⏱

> 2 lb (1 kg) beef or veal round, cut ¹⁄₂-in (1-cm) thick
> Salt and freshly ground black pepper
> 4 tablespoons vegetable oil
> ³⁄₄ cup (90 g) all-purpose (plain) flour
> 1 large onion, thinly sliced
> 3 garlic cloves, minced
> 1 small green bell pepper (capsicum), finely chopped
> 1 cup (260 g) chopped tomatoes
> 2 tablespoons chopped fresh parsley
> ¹⁄₈ teaspoon dried thyme
> Tabasco sauce to taste

Grits (right) and Grillades (left) in the courtyard of Brennan's.

Cut the meat into 3-in (8-cm) squares. Season with salt and pepper, then dredge in the flour and shake off any excess. Heat 2 tablespoons of the cooking oil in a heavy skillet over medium heat, brown the meat lightly, about 3 minutes per side, and drain on absorbent paper.

Make a roux in the same skillet with 2 tablespoons of the flour and the remaining 2 tablespoons oil, browning the roux until it's a rich dark color, about 20 to 25 minutes. Add 1¹⁄₂ cups (375 ml) water

and the onion, garlic, bell pepper, tomatoes, 1 tablespoon of the parsley, the thyme, and Tabasco sauce and simmer until the mixture thickens, about 15 minutes.

Return the meat to the pan, cover the skillet, and cook until tender, about 45 minutes for veal, 1 hour for beef. Stir often. Serve the grillades and sauce over hot grits. Garnish with the remaining 1 tablespoon parsley. Serves 6.

GRITS ⏱

> 1 teaspoon salt
> 1 cup (225 g) grits
> ¹⁄₄ cup (4 tablespoons) butter

Bring 5 cups (1¹⁄₄ liters) of water and the salt to a boil in a medium-sized saucepan, then gradually add the grits. Stirring constantly, reduce the heat and simmer until the mixture thickens, 5 to 10 minutes. Add the butter and stir until it is melted. Serves 6 (yields 5 cups, or 1¹⁄₄ liters).

CRAWFISH WITH SPICY AIOLI AND TOMATOES & GOAT CHEESE WRAPPED IN FILO

Dominique Macquet, Dominique's

CRAWFISH WITH SPICY AIOLI AND TOMATOES ☽☽

4 leeks, including the tender green leaves, chopped
1 tablespoon unsalted butter
1 lb (450 g) peeled crawfish (crayfish) tails, with liquid
1 red bell pepper (capsicum), diced
1–2 teaspoons chile powder
2 celery ribs, diced
1 large dill pickle, diced
1 medium-sized red onion, thinly sliced
½ tablespoon diced celery root (celeriac)
1 teaspoon paprika
1 teaspoon granulated garlic
3 tablespoons mayonnaise, homemade
1 egg yolk
1 tablespoon fresh lemon juice
1 cup (250 ml) peanut oil
6 thick slices vine-ripe tomato or garlic toast

Goat Cheese Wrapped in Filo (left) and Crawfish with Spicy Aioli and Tomatoes (right).

Sauté the leeks in butter over medium-high heat until golden, about 8 minutes. Then stir in the crawfish tails and bell pepper. Sauté until the liquid dries up, about 10 minutes. Stir in the chile powder, remove from the heat, and let cool.

In a food processor or blender, combine the celery, pickle, onion, celery root, paprika, garlic, mayonnaise, egg yolk, and lemon juice. With the motor running, slowly drizzle in the oil until fully incorporated. Fold in the crawfish mixture. Serve on slices of tomato, slices of garlic toast, or both. Serves 6.

GOAT CHEESE WRAPPED IN FILO ☽☽☽

10 white onions
11 oz (310 g) goat cheese
2 cups (500 ml) balsamic vinegar
1 cup (250 ml) honey
2 teaspoon chopped fresh thyme
4 sheets filo dough
¼ cup (½ stick, or 4 tablespoons) melted butter

The day before serving, slice the onions, place in a large skillet, and cook in their own juices on low heat for 4 hours, stirring occasionally. Let cool. The next day, cut the goat cheese into 6 portions. Over low heat, cook the onions for another 2 hours until they are soft and caramelized, then add 1 cup (250 ml) of the vinegar and ¾ cup (190 ml) of the honey. Reduce the liquid until it is syrupy, then let it cool. Add the chopped thyme.

Stack the filo, brushing each layer with butter. Cut the stack into 6 equal portions. Place one piece of the goat cheese in the middle of each piece of filo. Add about 1 tablespoon of the caramelized onion and wrap like a beggar's purse, lifting the corners and squeezing them together at the top.

Preheat the oven to 300°F (150°C, gas mark 2) and bake for 5 to 6 minutes, until golden brown. Dissolve the remaining honey in the remaining vinegar, then sprinkle this on the filo packets. Serves 6.

CRAWFISH BEIGNETS & CRAWFISH CARDINAL

CRAWFISH BEIGNETS

Don't worry if these savory tidbits remind you of conch fritters in the Caribbean: it's not the first or last time a food inspiration made its way up from the islands. In fact, locals sometimes refer to New Orleans as the "northernmost Caribbean island." No problem! ✆✆

1 cup (110 g) all-purpose flour
1 teaspoon baking powder
1 cup (250 ml) water
2 teaspoons chopped garlic
$^1/_2$ cup (90 g) chopped pimiento
3 scallions (spring onions), chopped
8 drops Tabasco sauce
1 pinch salt
8 oz (225 g) cooked crawfish (crayfish) tails
Vegetable oil for deep-frying
Lemon wedges

Crawfish Beignets (left) and Crawfish Cardinal (right).

In a bowl, combine all ingredients in the order listed, except the oil and lemon wedges. Cover the bowl with a damp towel and set aside for 30 minutes.

Preheat the oil in a deep-fryer or tall, heavy saucepan to 360°F (180°C). Drop the beignet batter by spoonfuls into the oil and fry until golden brown, 5 to 6 minutes. Do not fry more than a few fritters at a time. Drain and serve hot, garnishing each plate with a lemon wedge. Serves 4 to 6.

CRAWFISH CARDINAL

The allusion here is to a sauce as red as a Catholic cardinal's robe—neither the first nor the last time religion and cuisine operated on the same plane in New Orleans. In the spirit of true ecumenism, the same sauce works fantastically with shrimp, crabmeat, oysters—or all of the above. ✆

3 tablespoons butter
3 tablespoons all-purpose (plain) flour
2 tablespoons chopped scallions (spring onions)
$^1/_4$ cup (60 ml) white wine
1 cup (250 ml) milk
1 tablespoon tomato paste
Salt, ground white pepper, and ground red
    pepper (cayenne) to taste
$1^1/_2$ lb (680 g) peeled crawfish (crayfish) tails
French bread croutons

In a large skillet, blend together the butter and the flour, stirring for about 2 minutes. Then add the scallions, wine, and milk. Bring to a simmer. Stir in the tomato paste and season to taste with salt and the two peppers. Add the crawfish tails and simmer for 10 minutes.

To serve, spoon the crawfish and sauce into small bowls and garnish with French bread croutons. Serves 6.

BAKED OYSTERS

Arnaud's

So many New Orleanians start a meal with baked oysters that it almost seems mandatory. The process is always the same: Prepare a topping, preheat the oven to 400°F (200°C, gas mark 6), spoon the topping over raw oysters on the half shell, then bake for 7 to 10 minutes, or until the topping is heated through and golden. Then devour.

For a presentation that you would find in a restaurant, for each serving, fill a metal pie plate with rock salt. Set 6 oysters in the rock salt to hold them in place. Then top and bake. Set the pie plate on a dinner plate to serve. The following recipes yield enough topping for 36 oysters.

These baked oysters (left) and fresh oysters on the half shell (right) are served on French trompe l'oeil pieces created circa 1870. These decorative platters became popular during the Victorian era, when platters were even created for specific types of oysters.

OHAN TOPPING ⏱

1⅓ cups (315 ml) olive oil
3 large eggplant (aubergine) (about 4 lb, or
  2 kg), peeled and diced
¾ cup (45 g) chopped scallions (spring onions)
1 tablespoon dried thyme
1 teaspoon dried marjoram
1 teaspoon dried oregano
3 bay leaves
2 cups (520 g) diced tomatoes, undrained
1 teaspoon chopped garlic
⅓ cup (5 tablespoons) chopped fresh parsley
Salt and pepper

Heat the olive oil in a pot over high heat. Add the eggplant and sauté for 7 minutes. Add the scallions, thyme, marjoram, oregano, and bay leaves and sauté for 4 minutes. Add the diced tomatoes, bring to a boil, and simmer for 3 minutes.

Add the garlic and chopped parsley, cooking for 5 minutes more. Season to taste with salt and pepper.

Remove the bay leaves. Allow to cool completely before spooning atop the oysters and baking as directed above.

KATHRYN TOPPING ⏱

¾ cup (1½ sticks, or 170 g) butter
2¼ cups (400 g) finely chopped white onions
3½ cups (385 g) finely chopped celery
7½ cups (2 liters) artichoke bottoms or hearts,
  boiled and finely chopped
2 bay leaves
Ground red pepper (cayenne)
¾ cup (175 ml) sherry
3 cups (750 ml) Fish Velouté (page 41)
1 cup (125 g) unseasoned dry bread crumbs
Salt and white pepper

Melt the butter in a saucepan over high heat. Add the onions and celery, and sauté until transparent, about 5 minutes. Add the artichokes, bay leaves, and red pepper to taste, then add the sherry. Add the fish velouté and bring to a boil.

Reduce the heat and simmer for 4 minutes, then add the bread crumbs and stir until the mixture becomes a paste.

Season to taste with salt and white pepper, and remove the bay leaves. Allow to cool completely

before spooning atop oysters and baking as directed above.

Right: This nineteenth-century French or Austrian oyster plate has pearlized seaweed hand painted between the oyster wells.

SUZETTE TOPPING ⏱

10 tablespoons ($1^1/_4$ sticks, or 140 g) butter
6 slices raw bacon, chopped
$2^1/_8$ cups (130 g) finely chopped celery
$3^1/_2$ cups (325 g) finely chopped scallions
2 tablespoons finely chopped fresh parsley
$2^2/_3$ cups (450 g) chopped red pimientos
2 bay leaves
1 pinch dried whole thyme
Ground red pepper (cayenne) to taste
6 tablespoons brandy
$5^1/_3$ cups ($1^1/_4$ liters) Fish Velouté (page 41)
Salt and white pepper

Melt the butter in a saucepan over high heat. Add the bacon and sauté for 2 minutes, then add all the vegetables, herbs, and red pepper to taste. Cook for 3 minutes, then add the brandy and fish velouté. Boil for 2 minutes, then reduce the heat and simmer for 2 minutes.

Season with salt and white pepper. Remove the bay leaves. Allow to cool before spooning atop the oysters and baking as directed above.

OYSTERS ROCKEFELLER

This dish was created at Antoine's and so named because the sauce atop the oysters was so rich it was worthy of, well, Rockefeller. Antoine's has maintained a veil of secrecy over its recipe, but here's one variation that will produce similar magnificent results. ⏱

$1/_2$ lb (225 g) spinach
1 bunch celery
1 bunch scallions (spring onions)
1 fennel bulb
1 bunch parsley
$2^1/_2$ cups (5 sticks, or 570 g) unsalted butter
4 tablespoons Worcestershire sauce
2 tablespoons Pernod
Salt, black pepper, and ground red pepper (cayenne)

Finely chop the greens, then melt the butter and add the greens. Stir in the liquid ingredients, then season to taste with the remaining salt and both peppers. Preheat broiler (grill). Set 6 oysters on each of 6 pie pans filled with rock salt. Top each oyster with the vegetable mixture and place under the broiler (grill) until heated through, 5 to 6 minutes. Serve at once. Serves 6.

Using the oyster liquor, poach the bivalves until plump and opaque, about 5 minutes. Strain and set aside, reserving the cooking liquid from the process. Melt the butter in a saucepan and blend in the flour, cooking until the mixture becomes foamy, about 2 minutes. Add the wine and scallions, bring to a boil, and add the oyster liquor. Add the chopped parsley, season to taste, and simmer over low heat for 15 minutes. Carefully mix in the oysters and crabmeat, keeping the crab in lumps.

Preheat the oven to 400°F (200°C, gas mark 6). To finish the dish, spoon this mixture into ovenproof dishes or ramekins. Mix together the grated cheeses and bread crumbs, then sprinkle atop the oysters and crabmeat. Bake in the oven until the cheese is melted and the top begins to brown, about 10 minutes. Serves 8.

Left: This Limoges oyster plate, in an unusually deep shade of yellow, dates from the nineteenth century.
Below: The realistic fish on this starfish-shaped platter are characteristic of the Pallisy style circa 1870.

OYSTERS BONNE FEMME

There are several variations of this oyster dish anointed with the French phrase for "good woman." This recipe departs from the classic version along a path pioneered by Antoine's. One thing is certain: you'll thank the good woman, or the good man, who makes this for you. ⊘

3 dozen shelled raw oysters in their liquor
3 tablespoons butter
3 tablespoons all-purpose (plain) flour
$^{1}/_{2}$ cup (125 ml) dry white wine
$^{3}/_{4}$ cup (45 g) chopped scallions (spring onions)
1 tablespoon fresh chopped parsley
Salt and ground white pepper
1 cup (110 g) lump crabmeat
3 tablespoons grated Swiss cheese
3 tablespoons grated Romano cheese
$^{1}/_{4}$ cup (30 g) dry bread crumbs

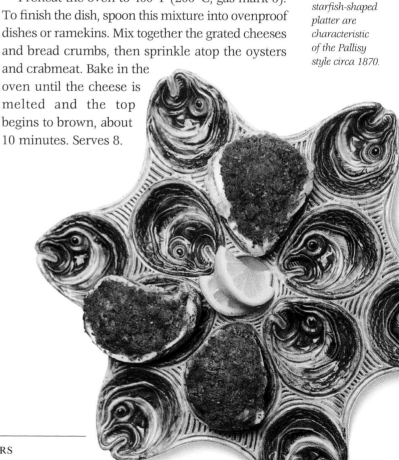

OYSTER-STUFFED ARTICHOKES & CRABMEAT RAVIGOTE

OYSTER-STUFFED ARTICHOKES

The influence of New Orleans' large Sicilian population is felt in any dish involving the stuffing of artichokes—and almost every restaurant has some such dish. Here's one that's both extra simple and extra good. ◑◐

1 tablespoon unsalted butter
4 scallions (spring onions), chopped
2 tablespoons all-purpose (plain) flour
2 dozen oysters
1 cup (250 ml) oyster liquor
6 fresh artichoke hearts, thinly sliced
2–3 teaspoons fresh lemon juice
Salt and black pepper
4 whole fresh artichokes
¹/₄ cup (25 g) Parmesan cheese

Prepare the whole artichokes. Trim off the top quarter of leaves. Snap off the bottom row of leaves. Cut the stem so the artichoke stands. Rub all of the cut surface with a lemon wedge. Steam the whole artichokes for 45 minutes or until tender. Drain them and set them aside to cool. When they are cool enough to handle, gently force open the leaves and remove the center leaves and the choke.

While the artichokes are cooking, melt the butter in a large skillet, add the scallions, and sauté. Stir in the flour until smooth, then add the oysters, oyster liquor, artichoke hearts, and lemon juice. Sea-son with salt and pepper. Simmer for 10 minutes, until the sauce thickens and the hearts are tender.

Preheat the broiler (grill). Spoon the artichoke and oyster mixture into the prepared artichokes, sprinkle with Parmesan cheese, and place under the preheated broiler (grill) for about 5 minutes, until the cheese turns golden brown. Serves 4.

CRABMEAT RAVIGOTE

Here's a simple starter with a French verb half-hidden in its name: *ravigoter*, or to invigorate. This New Orleans recipe is quite different from French ravigote sauces. ◐

1 cup (250 ml) mayonnaise
1¹/₂ tablespoons minced green bell pepper (capsicum)
1¹/₂ tablespoons minced scallions (spring onion)
1¹/₂ tablespoons minced anchovies
1¹/₂ tablespoons minced pimiento
4¹/₂ cups (510 g) lump crabmeat
Shredded lettuce

In a bowl, mix together all ingredients except the crabmeat and lettuce and chill in the refrigerator. Carefully blend the crabmeat with the chilled sauce, preserving the lumps. Chill mixture in the refrigerator. Serve atop shredded lettuce. Serves 6.

Crabmeat Ravigote (left) and Oyster-stuffed Artichokes (right).

SHRIMP AND TASSO WITH FIVE-PEPPER JELLY

Jamie Shannon, Commander's Palace

Here's a new-style starter that combines the peppery flavors of Louisiana pepper sauce with the sweet-pungent taste of pepper jelly. It's a country concept that definitely made it to town, judging by the elegance of its final form. ②②

Five-Pepper Jelly
- **6 tablespoons honey**
- **³/₄ cup (190 ml) white vinegar**
- **1 each red, yellow, and green bell peppers (capsicums), diced**
- **1 jalapeño pepper, diced**
- **¹/₄ teaspoon ground black pepper**
- **Salt**

Crystal Beurre Blanc
- **¹/₄ teaspoon minced garlic**
- **¹/₄ teaspoon chopped shallots**
- **2 teaspoons vegetable oil**
- **10 tablespoons Crystal hot sauce or other Louisiana hot sauce**
- **¹/₄ cup (4 tablespoons) heavy (whipping) cream**
- **1¹/₂ lb (6 sticks, or 680 g) unsalted butter, softened**

- **36 jumbo shrimps (prawns), peeled and deveined**
- **¹/₂ lb (225 g) tasso (see page 37), julienned**
- **1 cup (110 g) all-purpose (plain) flour seasoned with salt and pepper**
- **Vegetable oil**
- **36 pickled okra (ladies' fingers)**

To make the **five-pepper jelly,** pour the honey and vinegar into a pot and reduce over medium heat until sticky, about 5 minutes. Add the remaining ingredients and cook until the peppers are soft, 3 to 4 minutes. Add salt to taste.

Prepare the **crystal beurre blanc** by sautéing the garlic and shallots in a pan with the vegetable oil. Add the hot sauce and reduce by 75 percent, then add the cream and reduce the liquid by half. Whip in the butter a little at a time.

To finish the dish, make a ¹/₄-in (6-mm) incision down the back of each shrimp and place a strip of tasso in each. Secure with a toothpick. Lightly dust each shrimp with seasoned flour. Heat about 2 in (5 cm) of oil in a large skillet and fry the shrimp until golden.

Place the cooked shrimp in a bowl with the beurre blanc and toss until well coated. Spread the pepper jelly on the bottom of a small dish and arrange the shrimp, alternating them with pickled okra. Serves 8.

SHRIMP BAYOU LAFOURCHE

Andrea Apuzzo, Andrea's Restaurant

What happens when a Capri-born, European-trained chef adopts New Orleans as his home and comes into a delivery of picture-perfect local shrimp? Hopefully something like this reborn classic, named after an important bayou running along the eastern edge of Cajun Country. ☉

  2 tablespoons extra-virgin olive oil
  4 teaspoons chopped shallots
  2 teaspoons chopped garlic
  1 teaspoon crushed red pepper
  24 medium-sized shrimp (prawns),
      peeled and deveined but with tails on
  3 tablespoons brandy
  ½ cup (125 ml) dry white wine
  ½ teaspoon Worcestershire sauce
  Juice of 1 lemon
  1 teaspoon fresh rosemary leaves
  ½ teaspoon salt
  ¼ teaspoon ground white pepper
  Ground red pepper (cayenne)
  4 tablespoons unsalted butter, softened
  4 lemon wedges for garnish

Heat the olive oil in a large skillet over medium-high heat and sauté the shallots, garlic, and crushed red pepper until the shallots are transparent, about 3 minutes. Then add the shrimp and cook, turning once, just until they turn pink, about 3 minutes. Add the brandy, then remove the shrimp and keep them warm.

Add all the other ingredients to the skillet, except the butter, and simmer until the sauce is reduced by a third—about 10 minutes. Whisk in the butter. Return the shrimp to the pan and cook for 3 to 4 minutes more, coating them well with the sauce. Garnish with lemon wedges and serve. Serves 4.

SHRIMP RÉMOULADE

This dish comes in two colors around New Orleans —and either color is light years removed from the bland white or green versions found in France. This recipe tends toward the red, though in the local renditions pungent Creole mustard is the key. ☻☻

2 lb (1 kg) fresh medium-sized shrimp (prawns) in shell
1 large garlic clove, crushed
1 teaspoon black peppercorns, crushed
1 teaspoon salt

Rémoulade Sauce
2 tablespoons Creole mustard
1 tablespoon red wine vinegar
Salt and black pepper to taste
1 cup (250 ml) olive oil
1 tablespoon paprika
$\frac{1}{2}$ cup (60 g) finely chopped celery
1 cup (105 g) chopped scallions (spring onions)
1 teaspoon chopped garlic
$\frac{1}{2}$ cup (7 g) chopped fresh parsley
2 tablespoons freshly grated horseradish
$\frac{1}{8}$ teaspoon ground red pepper (cayenne)
2 tablespoons lemon juice

Romaine lettuce, shredded
8 tomato slices
Lemon wedges
Black olives

Put the shrimp in a saucepan with water to cover. Add the garlic, peppercorns, and salt. Gradually bring to a boil over medium heat. Simmer the shrimp for about 1 minute, remove from the heat, drain, and allow to cool. Peel and devein.

To prepare the **rémoulade sauce,** combine the mustard and vinegar with salt and pepper to taste in a mixing bowl, beating with a wire whisk. Gradually add the olive oil, whisking constantly. Then whisk in the remaining sauce ingredients. Mix the sauce with the peeled shrimp and set in refrigerator for at least 1 hour, though overnight is best.

When you are ready to serve, arrange the shredded Romaine lettuce and 1 tomato slice each on 8 salad plates. Spoon the shrimp and sauce onto the lettuce, and garnish with lemon wedges and black olives. Serves 8.

CHICKEN AND ANDOUILLE GUMBO

Away from the coast, a tradition grew up of using chicken to make a gumbo that could compete with the finest made with seafood. The two recipes have many similarities, of course, but time-honored differences, too. Here's a terrific chicken gumbo made with Louisiana's own andouille sausage. You'll also run into this dish called by the colorful name Gumbo Ya-Ya. ⊘⊘

1 5-lb (2½-kg) hen, cut into 10 pieces
Salt, ground red pepper (cayenne), and garlic
   powder
2½ cups (280 g) all-purpose (plain) flour
1 cup (250 ml) vegetable oil
2 cups (340 g) chopped onions
1½ cups (170 g) chopped celery
1½ teaspoons minced garlic
2 cups (340 g) chopped green bell pepper
6 cups (1½ liters) Chicken Stock (page 41)
1 lb (450 g) andouille sausage (or any spicy
   smoked sausage), chopped
Hot cooked white rice

Chicken and Andouille Gumbo (left) and Crawfish Bisque (right, recipe not included) shot on location at Tezcuco Plantation.

Season the chicken pieces with the salt, red pepper, and garlic powder; let stand at room temperature for 30 minutes. Place the flour in a large paper bag, add the chicken and shake until well coated. Reserve the flour.

In a large skillet, brown the chicken in the hot oil. Remove the chicken and set aside. When cooled, cut all meat from the bones and cut into chunks and set aside.

Using a wire whisk, loosen the browned particles from the bottom of the skillet, then stir in 1 cup (110 g) of the reserved flour. Stir constantly over medium-high heat until the roux is dark brown, 10 to 15 minutes.

Remove from heat and add the chopped vegetables, stirring to stop the roux from browning while cooking the vegetables for about 5 minutes. Transfer this mixture to a large pot, pour in the chicken stock, and bring to a boil. Lower the heat to a simmer; add the sausage and the deboned chicken. Continue cooking for 45 minutes over low heat.

Adjust seasoning with salt and pepper. Serve in soup bowls over steamed white rice. Serves 8.

SEAFOOD GUMBO

Commander's Palace

Gumbo comes from the African word *gombo*, referring to okra (ladies' fingers). The Choctaw Indians used ground sassafras leaves (filé) as a thickener for this stew instead of okra. ☉

Roux

$^3/_4$ cup (175 ml) vegetable oil
$^3/_4$ cup (90 g) all-purpose (plain) flour, sifted

4 large onions, diced
1 medium bunch of celery, cleaned and diced
4 green or red bell peppers (capsicums), diced
12 garlic cloves, minced
1 teaspoon cayenne pepper or 5 fresh cayenne peppers, diced
1 pinch oregano
1 pinch basil
1 pinch thyme
4 bay leaves
Salt and black pepper
8 cups (2 liters) Fish Stock (page 40) or cold water
$1^1/_2$ lb (675 g) gumbo crabs (hard-shelled tops off, lungs removed, and cut in half with claws cracked with the back of a knife)
2 links andouille sausage (about 1 lb, or 450 g), sliced in $^1/_4$-in ($^1/_2$-cm) pieces or any other smoked, firm sausage
1 lb (450 g) sliced okra (ladies' fingers)
1 lb (450 g) peeled medium shrimp (prawns)
1 quart (1 liter) shucked oysters in their liquor
Louisiana hot sauce

Place the oil in a large pot over high heat and heat the oil to the smoking point, about 5 minutes. Slowly add the sifted flour, stirring constantly until the mixture is the color of chocolate, about 3 to 5 minutes (timing will vary).

Once the roux is the right color, add the onions and cook them for one minute, then add the celery. Cook the celery for 30 seconds, then add the bell peppers, making sure to scrape the bottom of the pot. The aroma from this mixture should be wonderful.

Once the bell peppers have begun to soften, add the garlic, cayenne pepper, oregano, basil, thyme, and bay leaves. Season the mixture lightly with salt and black pepper.

Add the fish stock while stirring constantly. Then add the crabs, sausage, and okra. Bring the mixture to a boil, lower the heat, and simmer the mixture for about one hour, constantly skimming off any oil or impurities. After one hour the crab meat will look like white strings, when this happens, add the shrimp and cook them for 10 minutes. Then add the oysters and their liquor and bring the gumbo to a boil. Finish by adding your favorite Louisiana hot sauce, salt, and black pepper to taste.

Serve the gumbo over fluffy white rice. Serves 12 as an entrée.

TURTLE SOUP

Naturally, the key to making turtle soup is ground turtle meat, which is available in many New Orleans meat markets and especially in small, ethnic groceries. Ground veal works well as a substitute, but you can't call it turtle soup with no turtle in the pot. ☉

¼ cup (60 g) salt
1½ cups (340 g) fresh or frozen turtle meat
6 cups (1½ liters) Chicken Stock (page 41) or
   veal stock
2 garlic cloves, chopped
2 bay leaves
1 pinch dried whole thyme
3 tablespoons tomato paste
½ cup (60 g) chopped celery
1 cup (105 g) chopped scallions (spring
   onions)
½ cup (90 g) chopped onions
1 tablespoon chopped fresh parsley
1 lemon, cut in half
3–3½ tablespoons sherry
2 eggs, hard-boiled and chopped
Salt and white pepper
2 tablespoons roux (optional)

To cook the turtle meat, bring 4 quarts (liters) of water to a boil in a large pot with the salt and simmer the meat for 45 minutes. Drain off the water and chop the meat coarsely. Set aside until needed.

In a large pot, bring the chicken stock, garlic, bay leaves, and thyme to a boil. Add the tomato paste, vegetables, parsley, and lemon. Return to a boil, then reduce the heat and simmer for 10 minutes. Add the meat and the sherry, return to a boil, then reduce the heat and simmer for 5 minutes. Remove the lemon.

Add the eggs. Season to taste with salt and pepper. Thicken if desired by adding small amounts of roux. Serve in soup bowls, preferably with a final splash (about half a tablespoon) of sherry. Serves 6.

Helpful hint: New Creole cooks sometimes substitute alligator meat for the turtle. With more than one hundred 'gator farms in Louisiana, alligator is readily available. With either veal or alligator as a substitute, omit the first step of boiling the meat with the water and salt. Instead, add the meat when you add the sherry to the stock, and simmer the soup until the meat is tender, about 25 minutes, before adding the eggs.

LOBSTER BISQUE

Sazerac Restaurant, Fairmont Hotel

This classic French preparation has been a signature dish of the Sazerac Restaurant at the Fairmont Hotel for several decades. It is exceedingly rich, and lush and filling—something to keep in mind when planning any menu around it. At the restaurant, the soup always gets a final baptism with cognac at the table. ✪✪

Lobster Bisque, a signature dish of the Sazerac, served in its glowing dining room.

1 cup (2 sticks, or 225 g) unsalted butter
8 lobster shells
8 onions
4 fennel tops
1 celery rib
4 cups (1 liter) white wine
2 cups (500 ml) brandy
2 cups (500 ml) tomato paste
1 cup (90 g) white peppercorns

Roux
³⁄₄ cup (90 g) all-purpose (plain) flour
6 tablespoons vegetable oil or butter

Boiled lobster tails
Whipped cream
Cognac (optional)

Prepare a flavorful lobster stock by melting the butter in a large soup pot. Add the lobster shells and sauté for about 15 minutes, then add the vegetables, wine, brandy, tomato paste, and peppercorns. Stir for about 5 minutes, then add water to cover (1 to 2 cups, or 250 to 500 ml), and simmer for 3 hours. Cool and strain.

Make the light roux by mixing the flour and oil or butter together in a heavy-bottomed pan and cooking over low heat for about 10 to 12 minutes, until light brown.

To finish the bisque, heat the lobster stock and blend in the roux until the mixture coats a spoon. Chop the lobster meat. Serve the bisque in soup bowls, garnished with chopped lobster meat, a dollop of whipped cream, and cognac, if desired. Serves 6.

OYSTER STEW

Arnaud's

In the classic Creole restaurants, this might be upgraded on the menu to oysters stewed in cream. Yet at heart it remains a simple, hearty, warming soup constructed around Louisiana's succulent and salty bivalve. ✆

36 oysters
1 quart (1 liter) milk
2 pints (1 liter) half-and-half (half cream)
2 tablespoons ($^1/_4$ stick) butter
Salt and black pepper
Chopped fresh parsley

Shuck the oysters, reserving the liquor in the shells. Combine the milk and the half-and-half in a medium-sized pot, heating to just below scalding. Add the oysters with their reserved liquor and season with salt and pepper. Simmer for 5 minutes.

When ready to serve, ladle the oyster stew into bowls. Garnish with chopped parsley and a grind of black pepper. Serves 6.

OYSTER AND ARTICHOKE SOUP

This is one of those traditional dishes that no one remembers being without—yet whose rise to menu prominence is the work of a single chef, Warren LeRuth of the passionately remembered LeRuth's. The silky texture of this flavorful soup verges on the legendary. ◷

2 large artichokes
15 oysters, with their liquor
2 bay leaves
2 tablespoons unsalted butter
1 cup (100 g) chopped scallions (spring onions)
2 garlic cloves, minced
4 tablespoons all-purpose (plain) flour
$\frac{1}{4}$ teaspoon ground thyme
1 teaspoon salt
Ground white pepper
2 tablespoons lemon juice
Chopped fresh parsley

Place the artichokes in enough salted water to cover. Bring to a boil and cook for about 30 minutes or until tender. Remove from the water and cool. Peel off the leaves. Remove, slice, and set aside the hearts and bottoms.

In a large pot, bring 5 cups ($1\frac{1}{4}$ liters) of water to a boil, then add the oysters with their liquor and the bay leaves. Simmer over low heat for about 20 minutes.

Melt the butter in a separate pot, add the scallions and sauté until tender, about 3 minutes. Add the minced garlic followed by the flour, blending well. Pour in the stock and the simmering oysters. Continue stirring over medium heat until the soup thickens.

Remove 3 oysters, chop them fine, and return them to the pot, followed by the sliced artichoke hearts and bottoms. Season with the thyme, salt, and pepper. Add the lemon juice, sprinkle the top of the soup with parsley. Simmer for 10 minutes more. Serves 6.

JAMBALAYA & MAQUE CHOUX

JAMBALAYA

Jambalaya provides New Orleanians with a basic recipe into which they can toss in virtually anything from the refrigerator that's about to go bad. Don't worry if some people's jambalaya is dark brown while others' is brightest red—no two recipes are alike. ☉☉

2 lb (1 kg) ham, cubed
2 lb (1 kg) smoked sausage, sliced into coins
  $^1\!/_4$-in ($^1\!/_2$-cm) thick
1 large onion, chopped
$^1\!/_2$ cup (90 g) chopped green bell pepper
  (capsicum)
$^1\!/_2$ cup (7 g) chopped fresh parsley
2 celery ribs, chopped
5 garlic cloves, chopped
3 ripe tomatoes, chopped
1 teaspoon dried thyme
2 bay leaves
Salt and black pepper
2 cups (400 g) uncooked long-grain rice

Jambalaya (left) and Maque Choux (right).

In a heavy-bottomed skillet with a tight cover, brown the ham and sausage, then pour off the excess drippings. Add the onion and stir over medium heat until limp, about 3 minutes. Then add the green pepper, parsley, celery, garlic, tomatoes, thyme, and bay leaves. Season with salt and pepper.

Bring to a boil and cook, stirring, for about 5 minutes, then add the rice and $2^1\!/_2$ cups (625 ml) water. Cover and set over low heat for 25 minutes. Do not uncover until you check for doneness, near the end of cooking time. The dish is done when the rice is tender and all the liquid is absorbed. Fluff with a fork and serve. Serves 10.

MAQUE CHOUX

This dish was probably learned by the French from the Indians. ☉☉

16 ears fresh corn on the cob
1 tablespoon unsalted butter
1 tablespoon vegetable oil
1 cup (170 g) chopped onion
1 cup (170 g) chopped green bell pepper
  (capsicum)
1 teaspoon freshly ground white pepper
$^1\!/_2$ teaspoon ground red pepper (cayenne)
2 cups (520 g) chopped tomatoes
Salt
3 tablespoons heavy (whipping) cream

Using a sharp knife, cut the kernels from the cobs and scrape to obtain the milky pulp, producing about 8 cups (2 liters). In a skillet, heat the butter and oil, and cook the onion and green pepper until wilted, about 3 minutes. Add the corn and peppers, cooking until the corn starts to stick to the bottom, about 10 minutes. Add the tomatoes, salt, and cream. Cook until thick, about 10 minutes. Serve hot. Serves 10 to 12.

SOUFFLÉ POTATOES

Legend has it that these sublime "French fries" were created when a chef to the French king set out to greet the royal train with the royal fried potatoes. The train, however, was late, the potatoes were fried—and the chef was ready to lose his head. When the monarch arrived, the desperate chef plunged the cooked potatoes into oil that had been heating all this time, and they puffed up in the most extraordinary way. Now it's our turn: we lose our heads every time we nibble on Soufflé Potatoes, especially when they're dipped in lush béarnaise sauce. ①①①

   8 large Idaho potatoes
   4 quarts (liters) frying oil
   Béarnaise Sauce (page 40)

Peel and slice the potatoes $\frac{1}{8}$-in (3-mm) thick, preferably with a French kitchen device known as a mandoline. Heat the oil in the kettle to 300 to 350°F (150 to 180°C) and fry the potato slices in batches until they rise to the top of the oil, 1 to 2 minutes. Remove with a slotted spoon. Drain and cool to room temperature.

Just before serving, heat the oil to 425 to 500°F (220 to 260°C) and drop in the potatoes in small batches and cook until they are puffed and golden. Drain on absorbent paper, sprinkle to taste with salt, and serve with béarnaise sauce for dipping.

   Serves 4 to 6.

Helpful hint: With so much hot oil involved in the process, please be careful not to spill on, splash, or burn yourself.

SEAFOOD BOIL & BARBECUED SHRIMP

SEAFOOD BOIL

Whether you're boiling shrimp, crawfish, or crabs, be sure to do the whole New Orleans bit, from serving the shellfish dumped out on newspaper (even if not the local *Times-Picayune*!) to whipping up a cocktail sauce with a little too much horseradish and hot pepper sauce. That's the way we like it. ☉

1 cup (265 g) salt
1 lemon, sliced
$\frac{1}{2}$ bunch celery with leaves, chopped
2 large onions, chopped
$\frac{1}{2}$ bulb garlic, chopped
2 packages Seafood Boil (see page 36)
1 teaspoon ground red pepper (cayenne)
10 lb (4$\frac{1}{2}$ kg) medium-sized shrimp (prawns), with heads and shells on, well rinsed

Put everything but the shrimp in a large pot and fill the pot with water. Boil for 30 minutes to extract the flavor from the spices. Then add the shrimp. When the liquid returns to a boil, cook for 10 to 15 minutes, until the shrimp are firm and peel easily. When the shrimp are cooked, carry the pot to the sink, drain, and wash the shrimp with cold water to stop the cooking. Serves 5.

BARBECUED SHRIMP

This dish was created at a restaurant called Pascal's Manale—don't try to figure out the grammar; that's just what it's called. And speaking of what things are called, barbecued shrimp aren't barbecued at all. They're basically a festival of butter, garlic, and pepper, all longing to be sopped up with slices of French bread. ☉

1 cup (2 sticks, or 225 g) unsalted butter
1 tablespoon minced garlic
$\frac{1}{2}$ teaspoon ground red pepper (cayenne)
2 tablespoons freshly ground black pepper
1 tablespoon salt
4 lb (2 kg) large shrimp (prawns), preferably with heads and shells on, well rinsed
2 lemons

Divide the butter between 2 large skillets. Melt over medium heat, then add the garlic, peppers, and salt, dividing evenly into both skillets. Add half the shrimp to each pan and cook, turning frequently, until the shrimp are pink on both sides and firm, 4 to 5 minutes. Squeeze into the pans the juice of the lemons. Spoon the shrimp into bowls and serve with French bread. Serves 6.

Barbecued Shrimp (back, left) and Seafood Boil (front, right). The Greek Revival cottage of Tezcuco Plantation was built in 1855.

SEAFOOD FRIED IN CORNMEAL

The Cabin

Though the cooking times may vary slightly from seafood to seafood, the key here is frying at 375°F (190°C). That way the seafood is cooked before the batter gets too brown. ✆

1 lb (450 g) raw seafood (shucked oysters, peeled shrimp/prawns, fish fillets)
½ cup (60 g) cornmeal (maize meal), preferably yellow
½ teaspoon freshly ground black pepper
⅛ teaspoon ground red pepper (cayenne)
⅛ teaspoon paprika
Salt
Vegetable oil for frying
Cocktail sauce

Rinse the seafood and drain, keeping types separate. Pat dry. Combine the cornmeal with all ingredients, except the oil and the cocktail sauce. Blend well. Heat the oil in a skillet or fryer to 375°F (190°C).

Dredge the seafood in the seasoned cornmeal and drop a few at a time in the hot oil. Stir often, frying until golden brown, 1 to 2 minutes. Remove and drain on paper towels. Let the oil return to the proper temperature before cooking the next batch. Serve with cocktail sauce. Serves 2.

Fried catfish, frog's legs, shrimp, and soft-shell crab fried in cornmeal are specialties of The Cabin, which was originally a slave dwelling on the Monroe Plantation. The immense wooden alligator was carved from a huge cypress log.

SHRIMP CREOLE

The presence of tomatoes in a recipe is, in New Orleans, a sign that either Spanish or Sicilian cooks were in the kitchen on the day the dish was first made. In this case, the Spanish are prime suspects. ☺☺

2 tablespoons butter
1 large green bell pepper (capsicum), finely chopped
1 medium-sized onion, finely chopped
2 celery ribs, finely chopped
2 tablespoons all-purpose (plain) flour
1 large bay leaf
2 cups (520 g) chopped tomatoes
1 teaspoon Worcestershire sauce
$^1/_2$ teaspoon dried thyme leaves
$^1/_2$ teaspoon sugar
1 teaspoon salt
6 drops Tabasco sauce
2 lb (1 kg) shrimp (prawns), peeled and deveined
White rice, cooked

A lunch of Shrimp Creole and rice at Laura Plantation.

Melt the butter in a large, heavy skillet and add the bell pepper, onion, and celery. Sauté for about 5 minutes, until limp. Add the flour, stirring until brown. Add all other ingredients except the shrimp and rice. Stir until the mixture reaches a low boil and begins to thicken. Reduce the heat, cover, and cook for 30 minutes to blend the flavors.

Just before serving, add the shrimp to the sauce and stir just until they are pink but still firm, about 3 minutes. Remove the bay leaf and spoon the shrimp and vegetables over mounds of white rice. Serves 4 to 6.

POMPANO EN PAPILLOTE

From the famous Antoine's restaurant, this "pompano in a paper bag" recipe was created to honor a French balloonist, and it does indeed show a resemblance to a balloon. Be sure to slice open the bag right in front of the person who'll eat the pompano inside; the aromas are incredible. ☺☺☺

Sauce

1½ tablespoons butter
1 garlic clove, minced
1 tablespoon finely chopped parsley
1 tablespoon chopped scallion (spring onion)
1 shallot, minced
24 oysters, shucked
24 shrimp (prawns), peeled and deveined
2 teaspoons Creole seasoning
1 tablespoon all-purpose (plain) flour
4 cups (1 liter) Fish Stock (pages 40)
1 cup (250 ml) champagne
2 cups (500 ml) heavy (whipping) cream

4 8- to 10-in (20- to 25-cm) circles of
    parchment paper
4 tablespoons (½ stick) butter
8 6- to 8-oz (170- to 225-g) pompano fillets
16 medium-sized shrimp (prawns), peeled and
    deveined
16 raw oysters, shucked
¼ teaspoon Creole seasoning

To prepare the **sauce**, sauté the butter, garlic, parsley, scallion, shallot, oysters, shrimp, and Creole seasoning in a large sauté pan for 1 minute. Stir in the flour. Add the fish stock, champagne, and heavy cream. Bring to a boil. Reduce the heat to a simmer and reduce the sauce until thickened, 10 to 15 minutes. Reserve.

Preheat the oven to 350°F (180°C). Cut the parchment sheets into heart shapes and butter them on the inside. Spoon some sauce into the center of the 4 parchment hearts and set 2 pompano fillets on top of it. Set 2 shrimp and 2 oysters on top of each piece of fish, then sprinkle with Creole seasoning.

Carefully fold the paper in from the corners till it forms a sealed packet. Bake in the oven for about 15 minutes, until the parchment bags are puffed. To serve, cut open the top of each bag. Serves 4.

LOBSTER WITH SPINACH LEAVES

Dominique Macquet, Dominique's

A very luxurious lobster dish from an innovative New Orleans chef. ☺☺☺

5 lb (2½ kg) small Roma (plum) tomatoes, blanched and peeled
1 cup plus 1 tablespoon (265 ml) olive oil
¼ cup (50 g) minced garlic
2 tablespoons fresh thyme leaves

2 lb (1 kg) spinach leaves
10 shallots, diced
Salt and black pepper to taste
4 Maine lobsters, about 2 lb (1 kg) each, cooked

Sauce
2 onions, chopped
2 carrots, chopped
4 celery ribs, chopped
1 tablespoon Pernod
1 cup (225 g) crème fraîche
1 oz (30 g) caviar

Prepare the tomatoes in advance by spreading a sheet pan with ¾ cup (190 ml) of the olive oil, garlic, and thyme. Place the blanched, peeled tomatoes on the pan and season with salt and pepper. Bake in a 150°F (65°C) oven for 8 hours.

In a large saucepan, heat ¼ cup (65 ml) of the olive oil over medium-high heat and sauté the spinach with the diced shallots until the spinach wilts, about 2 minutes. Season to taste and allow to cool. Press the spinach into a strainer to remove all liquid. Make each of the 4 tians by alternating layers of spinach and tomato in a 3-in- (8-cm-) diameter metal ring, ending with spinach on top. You will not need all of the tomatoes and should have about 2 cups (500 ml) left for the sauce.

Remove the lobster meat from the shell, reserving the head and tail shell for garnish. Remove the gills from the head and discard. Reserve the coral.

Sauté the onions, carrots, and celery in the remaining 1 tablespoon of olive oil, then add the lobster coral and 4 cups (1 liter) water. Reduce by a third over high heat. Add 2 cups (500 ml) of the oven-dried tomatoes and reduce by half. Strain. Add the Pernod and the crème fraîche. Blend together.

To serve, place tians in the center of large dinner plates, carefully removing the metal rings. Add the lobster head facing the front of the plate and the tail in back. Place claw meat on both sides of the tian. Spoon the sauce onto both sides. Slice each tail into 8 medallions, 4 for each side of the plate. Spoon a small amount of caviar on top of each medallion. Serve immediately. Serves 4.

EGGPLANT CRABCAKES

Andrea Apuzzo, Andrea's

Crabcakes were popular in New Orleans long before they were the rage in restaurants around the United States—a testament to the quality of the crabmeat in these parts. In this local Italian variation, crabmeat is joined by eggplant for a savory celebration. ☺☺☺

2 whole medium-sized eggplants (aubergines)
Salt
2 tablespoons plus one 1 teaspoon olive oil
1 medium-sized onion, chopped
2 tablespoons chopped garlic
6 celery ribs, chopped
1 medium-sized leek, chopped
1 tablespoon fresh thyme leaves
1 tablespoon fresh marjoram leaves
¼ cup (65 ml) dry white wine
2 lb (1 kg) fresh crabmeat
1 teaspoon finely chopped pepperoncini
1¼ cup (75 g) fresh bread crumbs
½ cup (75 g) freshly grated Parmesan cheese
Lemon wedges

Preheat the oven to 400°F (200°C, gas mark 6). Cut the eggplants in half lengthwise, salt generously, and layer in a baking pan. Add 1 cup (250 ml) water. Bake until tender, 30 to 40 minutes. Set aside.

Heat 1 tablespoon of the oil in a nonstick skillet over medium-high heat. Add the onion and garlic and sauté until golden brown, about 10 minutes. Add the celery, leek, herbs, and white wine. Mix well and set aside.

With a spoon, remove the meat from the eggplant and mix briefly with the sautéed vegetable mixture in a food processor. Do not overprocess.

In another skillet, add 1 teaspoon of the olive oil, along with the crabmeat and a splash of white wine. Bring to a boil. Add the mixture from the processor, salt, pepper, and pepperoncini. Mix gently. Allow to cool.

Add 1 cup of the bread crumbs and the Parmesan cheese and mix together. Form into 8 patties and sprinkle each one with the additional ¼ cup (15 g) bread crumbs on the outside. Heat the remaining 1 tablespoon of olive oil in a skillet and sauté the patties for 2 to 3 minutes per side, until golden brown. Serve garnished with the lemon wedges. Serves 8.

Helpful hint: To save a little time, chop all the vegetables at once in a food processor before sautéing them.

CRAWFISH ÉTOUFFÉE

Greg Picolo, The Bistro

Here's a dish from Cajun Country that has taken New Orleans by storm. It should be robust and push your limits on pepper. *Étouffée,* by the way, means "smothered"—describing the cooking technique that makes these crawfish so good. ☻

Crawfish Étouffée at Laura Plantation.

½ cup (1 stick, or 110 g) unsalted butter
½ cup (60 g) all-purpose (plain) flour
¼ cup (65 ml) peanut oil
4 celery ribs, finely chopped
4 large onions, finely chopped
1 large green bell pepper (capsicum), finely
   chopped
4 tablespoons chopped fresh garlic
2 bay leaves, preferably fresh
6 fresh thyme sprigs or ½ teaspoon dried
3 tablespoons Worcestershire sauce
¼ teaspoon ground red pepper (cayenne)
4 cups (1 liter) Chicken Stock (page 41)
3 lb (1½ kg) crawfish (crayfish) tails, drained
   with liquid reserved
2 cups (500 ml) heavy (whipping) cream
Salt and black pepper
White rice, cooked
6 scallions (spring onions), chopped

Make a roux by combining the butter, flour, and oil in a heavy pan and cooking over low heat until a dark caramel color, about 15 to 18 minutes. Add all the vegetables except the scallions and cook until soft, 5 to 7 minutes. Add the bay leaves, thyme, Worcestershire sauce, and red pepper. Slowly pour in the stock, whisking to incorporate it into the roux.

Add the reserved crawfish liquid and cook over low heat for 1 hour, until no flour taste remains. Add the crawfish tails and the cream. Season to taste with salt and pepper. Cook for 5 more minutes and serve over steamed white rice. Garnish with chopped scallions. Serves 6 to 8.

GRILLED SCALLOPS
WITH WILD MUSHROOM GALETTE

Dominique Macquet, Dominique's

This terrific new dish is well worth the time it takes to make it. ⊘⊘⊘

Sun-Dried Tomato Paste

    1 cup (250 ml) sun-dried tomatoes (not packed in oil)
    $\frac{1}{2}$ cup (125 ml) dry white wine
    2 basil leaves
    $\frac{1}{2}$ cup (125 ml) extra-virgin olive oil

Red Pepper Vinaigrette

    2 red bell peppers (capsicums)
    $\frac{1}{2}$ tablespoon crushed garlic
    3 basil leaves
    1 cup (250 ml) extra-virgin olive oil
    Salt and black pepper

Wild Mushroom Galette

    2 oz (60 g) shiitake mushrooms, sliced, sautéed, and drained
    1 oz (30 g) oyster mushrooms, sliced, sautéed, and drained
    1 oz (30 g) morel mushrooms, sliced, sautéed, and drained
    $\frac{1}{3}$ cup (60 g) wild rice, cooked
    8 sheets filo dough
    14 tablespoons ($1\frac{3}{4}$ sticks) butter, melted

    24 scallops, seasoned with salt and pepper and brushed with olive oil
    24 fresh asparagus spears, trimmed
    Diced red pepper (capsicum)
    Diced scallions (spring onions)

Prepare the **sun-dried tomato paste** by rehydrating the tomatoes in the white wine, then draining and blending them in a food processor with the basil and the olive oil.

Prepare the **red pepper vinaigrette** by grilling or roasting the peppers until the skin is charred. Then put them in a paper bag for 5 minutes to allow the steam to loosen the skin. Peel and seed the peppers. Add the remaining ingredients and blend until smooth. Season to taste with salt and pepper.

To make the **wild mushroom galette,** mix together the sautéed wild mushrooms, the cooked wild rice, and the sun-dried tomato paste. Layer 4 sheets of filo with melted butter, then cut in half. Cut one half into 5 strips and place these into a 2-in (5-cm) metal ring, criss-crossing them. Add the mushroom mixture and close with the tops of the filo strips. Repeat the procedure with the remaining filo and filling to make 4 galettes. Preheat the oven to 300°F (150°C, gas mark 2) and bake the galettes for 10 minutes.

Grill the scallops until medium rare, 1 to 2 minutes per side. Blanch the asparagus spears and set 6 on each dinner plate like spokes of a wheel. Set a galette in the middle of each plate, then the grilled scallops between the spokes. Drizzle vinaigrette on each scallop. Garnish with diced red pepper and scallions. Serves 4.

BLACKENED REDFISH OR TUNA

Seldom in New Orleans is a dish so identified with a single chef as blackened redfish is with Paul Prudhomme. Yet this crusty "outdoor-tasting" entrée is created by making so much smoke that it really should be cooked outdoors. The fish fillet can dry out horrendously if not cooked fast enough and hot enough, so be faithful to the technique if you're going to try blackening at all. With redfish as scarce as it is, this dish is mostly made with tuna (as in this photo) or swordfish these days. ❶ ❶

Combine all the seasonings in a small bowl. Dip the fillets in the melted butter and liberally sprinkle the seasoning mixture on both sides. Heat a cast-iron skillet as hot as you can get it, till the color starts to lighten to gray on the bottom. Add 2 fillets.

Pour about 1 tablespoon of the butter on top of the fish. Be careful; it may flame. Cook the fish for only about $1\frac{1}{2}$ minutes on each side. Serve immediately. Serves 8.

George Rodrigue's famed Blue Dog looks on as Blackened Tuna is served at K-Paul's Louisiana Kitchen.

1 teaspoon salt
$\frac{1}{2}$ **teaspoon ground red pepper**
$\frac{1}{2}$ **teaspoon ground white pepper**
$\frac{1}{4}$ **teaspoon ground black pepper**
$\frac{1}{4}$ **teaspoon dried thyme**
$\frac{1}{4}$ **teaspoon dried basil**
$\frac{1}{4}$ **teaspoon dried oregano**
2 teaspoons paprika
8 8-oz (250-g) skinless, boneless redfish fillets, or swordfish or tuna fillets
$\frac{1}{2}$ **cup (1 stick, or 110 g) butter, melted**

REDFISH COURTBOUILLON

The French came up with the basic idea for this "short soup," pronounced "coo-be-yon" by the locals. The Creoles made the broth more substantial, almost a sauce served over the delicious whole redfish. If you can't locate redfish, substitute sea bass. ⊘⊘

1 tablespoon vegetable oil
1 medium-sized onion, finely chopped
3 large tomatoes, chopped
1 tablespoon tomato paste
$^1/_2$ cup (125 ml) red wine
$^1/_2$ teaspoon salt
$^3/_4$ teaspoon ground black pepper
1 4-lb (2-kg) redfish, cleaned with head
   removed

In a large saucepan over medium heat, heat the oil. Add the onions and sauté until limp, about 3 minutes. Then add the tomatoes, tomato paste, 1 cup (250 ml) water, and wine. Season with salt and pepper. Simmer, uncovered, until the sauce thickens, about 20 minutes.

Preheat the oven to 350°F (180°C, gas mark 4). Pour the sauce over the redfish in a large roasting pan and cook in the oven until cooked through, about 1 hour. Baste with the sauce occasionally. Serves 4.

SWEET POTATO REDFISH WITH KUMQUATS

Dominique Macquet, Dominique's

Now that you've enjoyed your redfish blackened and courtbouilloned, have a go at a newer treatment from one of the city's most innovative chefs. The combination of sweet potatoes and kumquats is a natural, even if nobody has ever tried it before. ◷

8 medium-sized sweet potatoes, peeled
Oil for deep-frying

Kumquat Beurre Blanc
   5 tablespoons olive oil
   3 shallots, diced
   1 lb (450 g) kumquats, chopped with skin on
   1 cup (250 ml) dry vermouth
   $\frac{1}{2}$ cup (1 stick, or 110 g) unsalted butter

   8 6- to 8-oz (185- to 250-g) redfish or red
     snapper fillets
Salt and freshly ground black pepper
Sliced kumquats (optional)

Slice the sweet potatoes lengthwise into $\frac{1}{4}$-in (6-mm) pieces. Soak in cold water to cover for about 20 minutes to remove the natural sugar.

To make the **kumquat beurre blanc,** heat 1 tablespoon of the olive oil in a small saucepan over medium-high heat. Add the shallots and kumquats and sauté until soft, about 5 minutes. Deglaze the pan with the vermouth, scraping up the brown particles from the bottom. Boil to reduce the liquid by half, then stir in the butter until the sauce is thickened and shimmering.

Preheat the frying oil to 375°F (190°C, gas mark 5). Dry the potato slices thoroughly, then deep-fry until they are crispy. Blend the fried potatoes in a food processor with the chopping blade until they look like cornflakes.

Brush the redfish with the remaining olive oil and season with salt and pepper. Sprinkle the potato flakes on the fish, then sear in a frying pan, about 1 minute on each side. To finish the cooking, cook the fish in a preheated 350°F (180°C, gas mark 4) oven for 5 minutes.

Arrange the redfish fillets on dinner plates and spoon the sauce around the sides. Garnish with additional kumquat slices, if desired. Serves 8.

TROUT AMANDINE & TROUT MEUNIÈRE

Arnaud's

TROUT AMANDINE

A close relative of Trout Meunière, this crisp and delicate fish dish has been a New Orleans favorite for decades. For a trendier variation, use pecans instead of almonds. Either way, you'll love the sweet, nutty taste. ⊘⊘

6 8- to 10-oz (250- to 300-g) speckled or brook trout fillets, or other firm, white-fleshed fish
1 cup (250 ml) cold milk
1 cup (110 g) all-purpose (plain) flour seasoned with salt and pepper
$\frac{1}{2}$ cup (1 stick, or 110 g) butter

Sauce

6 tablespoons ($\frac{3}{4}$ stick, or 90 g) butter
$1\frac{1}{2}$ cups (200 g) flaked almonds
$\frac{1}{4}$ cup (65 ml) fresh lemon juice
2 tablespoons chopped fresh parsley
Salt and black pepper

Trout Amandine (front) and Trout Meunière, served on Arnaud's mezzanine overlooking the main dining room.

Soak the fillets in the milk for about 10 minutes, then drain them and dredge them in the seasoned flour. Shake off any excess. In a heavy frying pan, melt the butter and fry the fish a few at a time until golden, about 5 minutes on each side. Place on a warmed platter and keep warm.

Prepare the **sauce** in the same pan by melting the butter and stirring in the almonds until they are lightly browned, about 4 minutes. Add the lemon juice, parsley, and salt and pepper to taste. Simmer for 2 to 3 minutes to reduce. Pour the sauce over fish. Serves 6.

TROUT MEUNIÈRE

This beloved standard of Creole cooking takes its name from the process of milling fine flour. What Creole chefs do with that flour, especially in the case of delicate trout fillets, is something else again. ⊘⊘

$2\frac{1}{2}$ cups (625 ml) peanut oil
6 8- to 10-oz (250- to 300-g) fillets fresh speckled trout, or other firm, white-fleshed fish
1 cup (110 g) all-purpose (plain) flour
$\frac{1}{2}$ cup (1 stick, or 110 g) butter
$\frac{1}{2}$ cup (125 ml) dry white wine
Salt and black pepper
1 lemon, sliced
$\frac{1}{2}$ garlic clove, finely chopped
6 parsley sprigs, finely chopped

Preheat the peanut oil to 350°F (180°C) in a heavy skillet. Dredge the trout in flour and fry 2 pieces at a time until golden, 5 to 7 minutes for each. Place on a platter and keep warm.

Melt the butter. Stir in the wine, season to taste with salt and pepper, and pour the sauce over the trout. Garnish with lemon slices, garlic, and parsley. Serves 6.

HONEY-ROASTED DUCK & CANDIED YAMS

Greg Picolo, The Bistro

HONEY-ROASTED DUCK

In the winter—and yes, even during football season—the men of New Orleans take to the marshes. The reason: it's duck season. ☻☻☻

3 2- to 3-lb (1- to 1½-kg) ducks
Salt and pepper
4 tablespoons (½ stick) unsalted butter
1 teaspoon ground red pepper (cayenne)
¾ cup (190 ml) balsamic vinegar
2 cups (500 ml) honey
1 teaspoon freshly chopped garlic
4 fresh thyme sprigs
2 tablespoons Worcestershire sauce
½ cup (125 ml) Cointreau or Triple Sec

Preheat the oven to 425°F (220°C). Season the ducks inside and outside with salt and pepper, then roast until rare, 40 to 45 minutes. Remove ducks from the oven, and cut lengthwise into halves. Discard the fat from the roasting pan and replace the ducks skin-side up in the pan.

In a saucepan, melt the butter and add the red pepper, vinegar, honey, garlic, thyme, Worcestershire sauce, and Cointreau. Cook over low heat for 5 to 7 minutes, then pour over the ducks. Roast 15 minutes more at 350°F (180°C, gas mark 4), until medium rare. Remove the ducks, let the meat rest, and keep it warm.

Honey-roasted Duck served with Candied Yams and wild rice, photographed at Tezcuco Plantation.

Skim the cooking liquid of any fat and reduce it slightly in a saucepan over high heat. Pour over the ducks and serve immediately with Candied Yams and Dirty Rice (page 135). Serves 6.

CANDIED YAMS☻

6 Louisiana yams (sweet potatoes), peeled and quartered
½ cup (110 g) firmly packed dark brown sugar
¼ cup (60 g) white sugar
Juice of 1 lemon
Juice of 1 large orange
¼ cup (½ stick, or 60 g) unsalted butter, melted
¼ cup (65 ml) brandy
2 tablespoons pure vanilla extract
Salt and black pepper
1 tablespoon cinnamon
½ teaspoon nutmeg

Preheat the oven to 375°F (190°C). Place all ingredients in a large Dutch oven. Add 8 cups (2 liters) water. Cover the pot and steam the yams in the oven until fork tender, 30 to 40 minutes. Remove the lid and reduce on the stove over high heat for 7 to 10 minutes, until the sauce is syrupy. Serves 6.

CRISPY SMOKED QUAIL SALAD

Susan Spicer, Bayona

This is one of Susan Spicer's best ideas for preparing game.②②②

4 quail, deboned

Marinade
- 1 tablespoon honey
- 1 tablespoon sweet soy (Indonesian ketjap manis) or hoisin sauce
- 1/2 cup (125 ml) peanut oil
- 1 tablespoon bourbon whiskey

Dressing
- 1 lb (450 g) quail or chicken bones
- 2 cups (500 ml) Chicken Stock (page 41)
- 2 tablespoons molasses
- 2 tablespoons cider vinegar
- 2 tablespoons walnut (or cider) vinegar
- 1/4 cup (50 g) chopped shallots
- 1 cup (250 ml) olive oil
- Salt and black pepper to taste
- 1–2 tablespoons bourbon whiskey

Spiced Pecans
- 1 tablespoon butter
- 1/2 cup (50 g) shelled pecans
- 1 teaspoon Worcestershire sauce
- 1/2 teaspoon salt
- 1/8 teaspoon ground red pepper (cayenne)
- 1 tablespoon sugar

Rice Flour Batter
- 1 cup (160 g) rice flour
- 1/4 teaspoon salt
- 1/8 teaspoon black pepper

Salad
- 1/2 lb (225 g) fresh spinach, cleaned and trimmed
- 1 ripe pear, thinly sliced
- 1/4 cup (65 ml) thinly sliced pickled red onion
- 1/2 cup (110 g) celery hearts and leaves, thinly sliced

Whisk together all **marinade** ingredients in a small bowl and add the quail. Let rest for at least 1 hour. Drain the quail and "cold-smoke" in a smoker for 30 minutes. The quail should still be mostly raw.

Prepare the **dressing** by browning the bones in a 350°F (180°C, gas mark 4) oven for 10 minutes, then placing them in a small pot and covering with the chicken stock. Bring to a boil, reduce the heat and simmer the stock until it reduces to 1/2 cup (125 ml) of syrupy liquid. Pour into a bowl and whisk in the molasses, vinegars, shallots, and oil. Season to taste with salt and pepper, then stir in the bourbon.

Make the **spiced pecans** by melting the butter in a saucepan and tossing with the nuts and all other ingredients. Spread on a small baking sheet and roast in a preheated 350°F (180°C, gas mark 4) oven for about 10 minutes, until lightly toasted.

Preheat frying oil in a deep-fryer to 350°F (180°C). Whisk together the **rice flour batter** ingredients with 3/4 cup (190 ml) water. Dip the quail in this batter and fry for 3 to 4 minutes, until golden brown. To make the **salad,** toss the fresh spinach with the dressing. To serve, top the salad with the quail, pear, pickled red onion, celery, and pecans. Serves 4.

CHICKEN BONNE FEMME

Though this name is sometimes applied to a version of Sicilian-style garlic chicken, here's a Creole version with much to recommend it. It's extremely easy to prepare. ⏀

4 chicken breasts, skinned and deboned
Salt and black pepper
¹/₂ cup (125 ml) olive oil
4 potatoes, peeled and sliced into thin rounds
¹/₂ lb (225 g) ham, diced
4 garlic cloves, minced
2 tablespoons chopped fresh parsley (optional)

Chicken Bonne Femme (left) and Sicilian Chicken (right).

Season the chicken breasts with salt and pepper. In a skillet, heat the olive oil over medium heat and sauté the chicken until it is light brown, about 4 minutes per side. Then remove it from the pan.

Add the potatoes, ham, and garlic to the skillet and sauté until soft, 10 to 12 minutes. Then return the chicken to the pan. Blend with the other ingredients and cook until done, about 10 minutes. Stir in the parsley, if using, for color and flavor. Use a slotted spoon to serve so the excess olive oil drains off. Serves 4.

SICILIAN CHICKEN

Here is a dish contributed by New Orleans' large and lively Sicilian population that has surely entered the mainstream. It is a festival of robust, southern European flavors. At Mosca's (a tumbledown food mecca on the west bank of the Mississippi) it's known as Chicken à la Grande, while other eateries surrender their own pride by dubbing it Chicken Mosca. ⏀

³/₄ cup (190 ml) olive oil
2 3-lb (1¹/₂-kg) chickens, cut up
¹/₂ teaspoon salt
1 teaspoon freshly ground black pepper
10 garlic cloves, mashed
1 teaspoon dried rosemary
1 teaspoon dried oregano
1 cup (250 ml) dry white wine

Heat the oil in a large skillet over medium heat. Add the chicken pieces and brown, about 5 minutes per side. Season them with salt and pepper, then add the garlic, rosemary, and oregano. Pour the wine over the chicken and simmer until the chicken is done and the liquid is reduced by half, about 1 hour. Serves 6.

MUFFULETTA

Here is the great Sicilian sandwich created at the French Quarter's Central Grocery and taking its name from the round, crusty loaf upon which it is constructed. Be sure to buy a top-quality olive salad or make one of your own. ☉

1 large round Italian bread loaf
Olive oil
3 slices Genoa salami
3 slices center-cut ham
3 slices Swiss cheese
3 slices Provolone cheese
6 tablespoons olive salad

Slice the loaf in half horizontally, creating a top and bottom. Brush olive oil on the inside of the bread. Arrange the cold cuts on the bottom half in the order listed, then top them with the olive salad.

Cut the sandwich into 4 wedges—or 2 if you are really hungry. Serves 2 to 4.

DAUBE GLACÉ

This famous Creole dish is to meats what calas are to desserts—seldom seen yet fondly remembered. It is a summer dish with similarities to hog's head cheese: light and full of flavor. ☉

¼ cup (65 ml) vegetable oil
3 lb (1½ kg) beef round
½ lb (225 g) salt pork
1 large onion, chopped
3 carrots, sliced
2 celery ribs, chopped
3 garlic cloves, minced
2 parsley sprigs, chopped
2 bay leaves
5 whole cloves
1 cup (250 ml) dry sherry
Salt and black pepper
1 packet (7 g) gelatin (gelatine)

A picnic under the trees at historic Oak Alley Plantation.

In a large skillet, heat the oil and sear the beef and pork. Then add 6 cups (1½ liters) water and all other ingredients, except the gelatin. Bring to a boil, then reduce the heat and simmer until the meat is tender, 2 to 3 hours.

Remove any bones from the meat and cut the meat into bite-sized pieces. Return it to the pot with the vegetables and liquid and simmer for 30 minutes more. Remove the bay leaves and cloves.

In a bowl, dissolve the gelatin in a spoonful of the pot liquid, then stir the mixture into the pot. Turn off the heat and let the daube cool before ladling into a 2-quart (liter) loaf pan.

Cover the pan with plastic wrap and refrigerate for at least 4 hours before serving. Unmold onto a platter and cut into slices. Serve cold. Serves 8.

BRONZED VEAL CHOPS IN A CHIPOTLE CREAM

Paul Prudhomme, K-Paul's Louisiana Kitchen

Chipotle Cream ⓐ ⓑ

- $\frac{1}{4}$ lb (125 g) plus 2 tablespoons unsalted butter, in all
- 2 cups (240 g) chopped onions
- $2\frac{1}{2}$ teaspoons ground dried chipotle chile peppers
- $3\frac{1}{4}$ teaspoons Chef Paul Prudhomme's Meat Magic®, in all
- 1 cup (250 ml) chicken or beef stock (pages 40, 41)
- 4 oz (110 g) wild mushrooms, sliced thinly
- 2 cups (500 ml) heavy (whipping) cream
- $\frac{1}{4}$ teaspoon salt
- $\frac{1}{2}$ teaspoon light brown sugar

Veal Chops

- 2 tablespoons vegetable oil
- 6 10-oz (285-g) veal chops, each about 1-in ($2\frac{1}{2}$-cm) thick
- 2 tablespoons Chef Paul Prudhomme's Meat Magic®

To prepare the **chipotle cream,** place $\frac{1}{4}$ lb (125 g) of the butter in a 10-in (25-cm) nonstick skillet over medium-high heat. When the butter begins to sizzle, add the onions. Cook, stirring frequently, until the onions have turned a light brown, about 15 minutes. Add the chipotle and 1 tablespoon of the Meat Magic®. Cook, stirring constantly, until the seasonings have darkened slightly, about 2 to 3 minutes. Add the chicken or beef stock; scrape the bottom of the skillet to loosen any brown crust on the skillet bottom. Bring to a boil, then simmer for 5 minutes, stirring frequently. Remove from the heat, then purée the mixture in a food processor or blender. Set aside.

Add 1 tablespoon of the remaining butter to the skillet and place over high heat. When the butter sizzles, add the mushrooms and remaining Meat Magic® and sauté until the mushrooms begin to darken, about 3 minutes. Return the purée to the skillet, bring to a boil, then reduce the heat to medium. Add the cream, salt, and sugar. Bring to a boil, simmer for 5 minutes. Whisk in the remaining tablespoon of butter. Set the sauce aside (yields about 4 cups, or 1 liter) and prepare the chops.

To prepare the **veal chops,** season each veal chop evenly with $\frac{1}{2}$ teaspoon of the Meat Magic® per side, patting it in gently with your hands.

Heat the oil in a large heavy skillet until the oil is smoking hot, 5 to 7 minutes. Put 2 or 3 of the chops in the hot skillet. (When bronzing, it is important not to crowd the pan. Always leave plenty of space between the chops). Cook, turning once, until the chops are brown on the outside but still very rare in the center, about 1 to 2 minutes. Place the chops in a 500°F (250°C, gas mark 10) oven for 3 to 4 minutes to finish. Repeat the process for the remaining chops.

Serve 1 chop per person, topped with $\frac{1}{2}$ cup (125 ml) of the sauce. Makes 6 servings.

BEEF FILETS WITH MARCHAND DE VIN SAUCE & PANEED VEAL

BEEF FILETS
WITH MARCHAND DE VIN SAUCE

Named after the French wine merchants who created the sauce using their own wines, this dish is immensely popular in the grand Creole palaces. New Orleanians, as usual, tend to like more garlic than is found in the original recipe from France. ☉

Marchand de Vin Sauce (page 41)
$^1/_4$ cup (65 ml) vegetable oil
Salt and freshly ground black pepper
6 beef filets

Prepare the **marchand de vin sauce** as directed on page 41. Keep the sauce warm.

To prepare the filets, combine the oil with salt and pepper to taste, then rub the filets with it. Cook them in a preheated skillet to the desired degree of doneness, from about 5 minutes on each side for rare to 10 minutes for well-done. Serves 6.

PANEED VEAL

Only a generation ago, this dish (pronounced pan-aid) was known simply as "paneed meat" and cooked all over New Orleans because veal was less expensive than beef. Those were the days! ☉

6 $^1/_4$-in- (6-mm-) thick veal cutlets
Salt and black pepper
1 egg, beaten with 1 tablespoon of water
1 cup (125 g) dry bread crumbs
1 tablespoon vegetable oil
1 tablespoon butter
Lemon wedges

Using a mallet, pound the veal cutlets until they are thin and tender and season them with salt and pepper. Dip in the egg mixture, then in the bread crumbs, then back in the egg mixture.

Heat the oil and butter in a heavy skillet and sauté the meat on both sides until golden brown. Drain on absorbent paper. Serve with lemon wedges. Serves 6.

Paneed Veal (left) and Beef Filets with Marchand de Vin Sauce (right).

BANANAS FOSTER

Brennan's

This has to be the single most famous dessert in New Orleans, though by no means the only magnificent one. It was devised at Brennan's for a good customer named Foster, who happened to own a local awning company. Now Mr. Foster is much more famous for flaming bananas than for shading windows from the summer sunshine. ☺

4 teaspoons ground cinnamon
3 teaspoons sugar
6 tablespoons (³/₄ stick) butter
3 cups (680 g) firmly packed light brown sugar
6 ripe bananas, peeled and quartered
¹/₃ cup (80 ml) dark rum
¹/₃ cup (80 ml) banana liqueur
6 scoops vanilla ice cream

Mix together the cinnamon and white sugar and set aside. In a flambé pan, mash together the butter and brown sugar, then set the pan over a flame until the mixture melts. Add the bananas flat-side down and heat for about 1 minute.

Remove the pan from the flame to add the rum, then return it to the heat and ignite the alcohol. Sprinkle the cinnamon-sugar mixture into the flame. When the fire burns down, remove the pan from the heat and add the banana liqueur, then return to the heat and ignite again. Mix well.

Place one scoop of ice cream in each of 6 champagne glasses, cover with the hot banana mixture and serve immediately. Serves 6.

BREAD PUDDING WITH WHISKEY SAUCE

Arnaud's

The existence of this dish has everything to do with the amount of French bread consumed around New Orleans every day—and the amount in danger of being wasted when the fresh loaves come in. Fear not—early Creole chefs reworked an old European technique of turning drying bread into a dazzling dessert. Here's how. ☺☺

1 loaf French bread
1 quart (liter) milk
3 eggs, beaten
2 cups (450 g) sugar
2 tablespoons vanilla extract
1 cup (140 g) raisins
4 tablespoons unsalted butter, melted

Whiskey Sauce

$^1/_2$ cup (1 stick, or 110 g) unsalted butter, softened
1 cup (225 g) sugar
1 egg, beaten
1 tablespoon whiskey

Bread Pudding with Whiskey Sauce (left) and a Crème Brulée (right, recipe on page 136). This straw boater is a timeless example of New Orleans elegance.

Preheat the oven to 300°F (150°C, gas mark 2). Break up the French bread into small cubes and set in the milk to soak until the bread absorbs all of the milk. Then add the eggs, sugar, vanilla, and raisins. Stir well. Pour the melted butter into a 2-quart (liter) baking pan, add the bread mixture, and bake until a knife inserted in the center comes out clean, about 1 hour. Let cool.

Prepare the **whiskey sauce** by creaming together the butter and sugar, heating in a double boiler until hot and well dissolved. Rapidly whip in the egg, avoiding curdling. Let the sauce cool and add the whiskey.

Cut the bread pudding in cubes and place on 6 individual serving dishes. Gently heat the sauce and spoon over the top of each serving. Serves 6.

CUP CUSTARD & CHERRIES JUBILEE

CUP CUSTARD

This popular dessert is a close relative of the Spanish flan—and may have even arrived in town during Spain's brief but influential domination. ✇

3 eggs
$^1/_2$ cup (110 g) sugar
2 cups (500 ml) milk
$1^1/_2$ teaspoons vanilla extract
$^1/_2$ teaspoon vegetable oil
$^1/_2$ teaspoon freshly grated nutmeg

Caramel Sauce
1 cup (225 g) white sugar
1 cup (250 ml) boiling water

In a bowl, beat the eggs and sugar until creamy. Heat the milk in a pan to the scalding point, then pour the milk slowly into the egg mixture, beating constantly. Stir in the vanilla.

Preheat the oven to 350°F (180°C, gas mark 4). Spread the vegetable oil over the bottom and sides of 4 individual baking cups. Pour the custard through a strainer into the cups and sprinkle the top with the nutmeg. Place the cups in a large roasting pan and add enough hot water to the pan to reach halfway up the sides of the cups.

Bake until a knife inserted into the center of a custard comes out clean, 25 to 30 minutes. Remove from oven and allow to cool. Cover and refrigerate.

To make the **caramel sauce,** pour the sugar into a small, heavy-bottomed pan. Place over low heat and cook, without stirring, until the sugar melts and turns a light brown. Watch closely to avoid burning the sugar, and shake the pan from time to time. When the sugar is completely melted, stir in the boiling water, working quickly and wearing two oven mitts to protect your hands from splatters. Continue cooking and stirring for 3 to 4 minutes. Remove from the heat and cool.

To serve, pour the cooled sauce over the chilled custard. Serves 4.

CHERRIES JUBILEE

Like Bananas Foster, here is a dessert born from the heart of celebration, New Orleans-style. ✇

$1^1/_2$ cups (375 ml) brandy
$^1/_2$ cup (110 g) sugar
2 pints (1 liter) fresh or canned pitted cherries
6 scoops vanilla ice cream

In a saucepan, heat the brandy with the sugar until the sugar is dissolved, then add the cherries. Ignite the liquid carefully with a long-stemmed match and stir the cherries until the fire burns out.

Scoop ice cream into 6 dessert bowls, then cover the ice cream with the cherries and their sauce. Serve immediately. Serves 6.

Cup Custard (left) and Cherries Jubilee (right). The blood-red jubilee is a particularly appropriate dessert to enjoy in the beautiful Garden District home of Anne Rice, author of bestselling novels on vampires who live in New Orleans.

BUTTERMILK PIE

The Cabin

The buttermilk gives this custard pie extra richness and a slight tang. ⏱

2 cups (450 g) sugar
1 teaspoon ground cinnamon
1 teaspoon ground nutmeg
1 teaspoon vanilla extract
2 tablespoons cornstarch
½ cup (110 g, or 1 stick) butter, melted
3 large eggs, at room temperature
1 cup (250 ml) buttermilk, at room temperature
Unbaked 9-in (23-cm) pie shell

Buttermilk pie in the rustic surroundings of The Cabin.

Preheat the oven to 350° F (180°, gas mark 4). In the bowl of an electric mixer, combine the sugar, spices, vanilla, cornstarch, butter, and eggs. Beat on slow speed until the batter is blended and uniform. Add the buttermilk and mix well. Pour into an unbaked 9-in (23-cm) pie shell. Bake until set and brown on top, about 40 minutes. Serves 8.

PECAN PIE

Like every other corner of the Deep South, New Orleans loves its pecan pie. This recipe includes making the pie crust, though frozen and refrigerated crusts can be quite satisfactory. ②②

Crust
1/3 cup (5 tablespoons) solid shortening (butter)
1 cup (110 g) all-purpose (plain) flour
1/2 teaspoon salt
2 1/2 tablespoons water

Filling
1/2 cup (110 g) firmly packed brown sugar
1 tablespoon cornstarch
3 eggs, beaten
1 cup (250 ml) dark corn (golden) syrup
1 cup (250 ml) light corn (golden) syrup
2 tablespoons vanilla extract
1 1/2 cups (150 g) pecan pieces
Pecan halves

Preheat the oven to 350°F (180°C, gas mark 4). To make the **crust,** mix the shortening and the flour, then add the water. Mix well, form into a ball and return to the bowl. Cover the bowl and refrigerate the mixture for 30 minutes. Roll out the dough and place in an 8-in (20-cm) pie plate. Trim and crimp the edges.

To make the **filling,** blend the sugar, cornstarch, and eggs in the bowl of an electric mixer. Then add both syrups and the vanilla, mixing thoroughly. Place the pecan pieces atop the pie crust, add the filling and bake for 40 minutes or until a knife inserted in the filling comes out clean. Let the pie cool. Garnish as desired with pecan halves. Serves 8.

PRALINES AND CALAS

PRALINES

Pralines are one of those sweets that came to prominence as French Quarter street food. Now they are sold in tourist shops all over the Quarter—a less romantic system than the strolling vendors of yore—and shipped all over the world. ②

1½ cups (340 g) firmly packed dark brown
    sugar
1½ cups (340 g) white sugar
2 tablespoons butter
⅛ teaspoon salt
1½ cups (375 ml) evaporated milk
2 cups (200 g) shelled pecan halves
1 teaspoon vanilla extract
1 teaspoon vegetable oil

A snack of Calas (in dish) and Pralines (front) at Nottoway Plantation.

In a large saucepan, combine all the ingredients in a heavy-bottomed saucepan and cook over medium heat, stirring with a wooden spoon. Cook at a low boil for about 4 minutes (a candy thermometer should register 260°F, or 127°C), or a drop of the mixture should form a "hard ball" when dropped into cold water). Remove the saucepan from the heat. Beat the mixture until it cools and becomes creamy, about 2 minutes.

Form the pralines by dropping a tablespoon of the pecan mixture onto large pieces of aluminum foil or waxed paper. Let the candies cool thoroughly before storing them in an airtight container. Makes about 40 candies.

CALAS

These sweet rice cakes, pronounced "cal-lah," are seldom served anymore, but are fondly remembered. People remember—or remember being told of—the bandanaed vendors who swirled through the French Market shouting "beau calas!" ② ②

2 tablespoons granulated sugar
2 eggs
1 teaspoon vanilla extract
2 teaspoons baking powder
½ teaspoon salt
2 cups (225 g) sifted all-purpose (plain) flour
1 cup (200 g) cooked white rice
Vegetable oil for deep-frying
Powdered sugar or cane (golden) syrup

In a mixing bowl, beat together the sugar, eggs, and vanilla until foamy and bright yellow. Then add 1½ cups (375 ml) water and beat well. In a separate bowl, combine the baking powder and salt with the flour. Blending with a wire whisk, add this to the egg mixture. Add the rice, coating every kernel. Divide the dough into 6 portions and moisten your hands with a small amount of vegetable oil. Gently form 6 balls of dough and set aside on waxed paper.

Heat about 1 in (2½ cm) of oil in a heavy skillet to 365°F (180°C). Slowly lower the rice balls into the hot oil with a slotted spoon, frying until a golden crust develops. Turn to keep from burning. Serve immediately with powdered sugar or cane syrup. Serves 6.

COCKTAILS

Sazerac Bar, Fairmont Hotel

SIMPLE SYRUP

1 cup (250 ml) water
2 cups (450 g) sugar

In a heavy-bottomed saucepan, combine the water and sugar and stir to dissolve. Bring to a boil and boil for 5 minutes. Cool, then store in a jar in the refrigerator and use as needed. Yields about 1 cup (250 ml).

GIN FIZZ

1½ fl oz (45 ml) gin
2 drops orange flower water
1 egg white
1 tablespoon Simple Syrup (see above)
½ teaspoon lemon juice
2 fl oz (60 ml) half-and-half (half cream)
2 fl oz (60 ml) milk

Lined up on the Sazerzac Bar are, clockwise from far left, Mint Julep, Hurricane, Absinthe Suissesse, Brandy Milk Punch, Crème de Menthe, Sazerac, and Crème de Noya.

Combine all ingredients in a shaker with ice. Shake vigorously for 30 seconds. Pour over ice cubes in a chilled champagne glass.

BRANDY MILK PUNCH

1½ fl oz (40 ml) brandy
1 tablespoon Simple Syrup (see above)
6 drops vanilla extract
2 fl oz (60 ml) half-and-half (half cream)
2 fl oz (60 ml) milk
Ground nutmeg

Combine all the ingredients except the nutmeg in a shaker with ice. Shake well, then strain into a chilled highball glass with a little ice. Then dust with nutmeg.

ABSINTHE SUISSESSE

1½ fl oz (45 ml) Herbsaint liqueur
1 egg white
3 drops orange flower water
3 drops white crème de menthe
1 tablespoon Simple Syrup (see above)
2 fl oz (60 ml) half-and-half (half cream)
2 fl oz (60 ml) milk

Combine all the ingredients in a shaker with ice. Shake vigorously until frothy, then strain into a chilled stem glass with a little crushed ice.

SAZERAC

2 fl oz (60 ml) rye whiskey
1 teaspoon Simple Syrup (see above)
3 dashes Peychaud's bitters
3 dashes Angostura bitters
Splash of water
2 dashes Herbsaint liqueur
Lemon twist

Combine all the ingredients, except the Herbsaint and lemon twist, with ice. Pour the Herbsaint into a chilled rock (or old-fashioned) glass and coat the interior of the glass. Pour off any excess. Strain the rye mixture into the glass and add the lemon twist.

MINT JULEP

6 mint leaves
2 teaspoons powdered sugar
2 fl oz (60 ml) bourbon
Crushed ice
Mint sprig

In the bottom of a tall highball glass, combine the mint leaves with the sugar. Using a spoon, crush the leaves in the sugar, then add the bourbon. Fill the glass with crushed ice and garnish with the mint sprig. Serve with a cocktail straw.

HURRICANE

2 fl oz (60 ml) Red Passion fruit cocktail mix, available commercially
2 fl oz (60 ml) fresh lemon juice
4 fl oz (120 ml) dark rum
1 orange slice
1 maraschino cherry

Fill a tall, curved Hurricane glass with crushed ice. Add the cocktail mix, lemon juice, and rum. Decorate with an orange slice and cherry.

CAFE BRÛLOT

2 tablespoons whole cloves
14 cinnamon sticks, broken
2 tablespoons sugar
Peel of 1 lemon
1 orange
$\frac{1}{2}$ cup (125 ml) plus 1 tablespoon Grand Marnier
$\frac{1}{3}$ cup (80 ml) plus 1 tablespoon French brandy
4 cups (1 liter) hot, freshly brewed black coffee

In a brûlot bowl (or stainless-steel or silver bowl), place the cloves, cinnamon sticks, sugar, and lemon peel. Peel the orange carefully in 1 long strip, leaving the peel attached at one end. Stud the orange peel with the cloves, recoil the peel around the orange, and place it in the brûlot bowl.

Add the $\frac{1}{2}$ cup (125 ml) Grand Marnier and the $\frac{1}{3}$ cup (80 ml) brandy, then set the bowl over a flame to heat the ingredients. Press a fork into the pulp of the orange, lifting it out of the bowl and setting it aside.

Pour the remaining tablespoon of Grand Marnier and tablespoon of brandy into a stainless-steel or silver ladle and ignite carefully using a long-stemmed match. With your free hand, pick up the orange on the fork and turn it so the clove-studded peel twists down into the liquid in the bowl.

Dim the lights in the room. Pour the flaming alcohol from the ladle down the peel. Twice scoop the ladle into the bowl for more of the now-flaming liquid, pouring it down the peel. When all flames burn out, pour the coffee into the bowl. Discard the orange and ladle the drink into New Orleans brûlot cups or any decorative coffee cups. Serves 6.

Additional Recipes

RED BEANS AND RICE

Photograph on page 4

It's Monday in New Orleans—and the predominant smell is red beans cooking. Well, times have changed a bit from the days when Monday existed for putting on a big pot of red beans and doing the week's laundry. But since people still wonder what Monday is for, red beans tend to be on that day's menus in even the fanciest restaurants. They are most often served with a side of spicy smoked sausage. ♪♪

1 lb (450 g) dried red kidney beans
1 large onion, chopped
1 lb (450 g) pickled pork or ham, cut in cubes
1 bay leaf
4 garlic cloves, minced
$^1/_3$ cup (5 tablespoons) chopped fresh parsley
Salt and black pepper
Hot cooked white rice
Louisiana smoked sausage

Wash the beans and soak them in water to cover overnight. Drain away the water and put the beans in a large kettle. Cover them with the 8 cups (2 liters) of fresh water, cover the pot and boil for 1 hour over low heat. Add the onion and pork or ham, partially cover the pot, and cook until the meat is tender, about $1^1/_2$ hours.

Add the bay leaf, garlic, and parsley. Season to taste with salt and pepper, then cook, with the lid ajar, for about 30 minutes more, until the beans start to turn creamy. Serve over white rice with strips of smoked sausage on the side. Serves 6.

CORN BREAD ♪

Photograph on page 4

1 cup (110 g) sifted all-purpose (plain) flour
$1^1/_2$ cups (260 g) sifted cornmeal (maize meal)
1 teaspoon baking soda
$^1/_2$ teaspoon salt
2 eggs
1 cup (250 ml) buttermilk
2 cups (500 ml) whole milk
$1^1/_2$ tablespoons butter

Preheat the oven to 350°F (180°C, gas mark 4). In a mixing bowl, sift together the flour, cornmeal, baking soda, and salt. Beat the eggs until foamy and stir into the dry mixture. Stir in the buttermilk and 1 cup (250 ml) of the whole milk.

In a large cast-iron or ovenproof skillet, heat the butter. When it is hot but not yet brown, pour in the batter along with the remaining milk. Do not stir. Place the skillet in the oven and bake until cooked through, about 50 minutes. Slice into wedges. Serves 8.

BARBECUED OYSTERS
Mike Fennelly, Mike's on the Avenue

Photograph on page 27

This New Creole dish, finished outdoors on a grill, intriguingly blends several familiar local presentations with a Mediterranean element not usually encountered. Like so many of chef Mike Fennelly's best creations, this dish shows a powerful Asian influence as well. ⊘ ⊘

2 tablespoons tomato paste
2 garlic cloves
2 shallots
2 teaspoons minced red onion
2 teaspoons minced fresh cilantro (coriander)
$1/2$ teaspoon toasted Szechuan peppercorns
2 teaspoons mild chili, minced
$2^{1}/_{2}$ tablespoons white vinegar
$1/3$ cup (75 g) firmly packed brown sugar
$1/3$ cup (80 ml) sesame oil
4 teaspoons freshly grated ginger
$1/2$ teaspoon ground red pepper (cayenne)
Juice of $1^{1}/_{2}$ lemons
$1/2$ cup (125 ml) teriyaki sauce
$1/3$ cup (80 ml) soy sauce
3 dashes hot pepper sauce
$1/2$ lb (225 g) pancetta, thinly sliced
2 dozen oysters in the shell

Blend all ingredients, except the pancetta and oysters, until smooth. Place the pancetta on a cookie sheet and roast in a 350°F (180°C, gas mark 4) oven for 2 to 3 minutes, until lightly browned. Pat dry with a paper towel and cut into $1/4$-in (6-mm) squares.

Prepare a hot fire in a grill. Shuck the oysters and discard the top half of the shell. Rinse to remove shell particles. Place the oyster on the half shell over hot coals and pour some of the sauce over each oyster. Sprinkle with the pancetta. Grill for 5 to 7 minutes, or until bubbly. Serves 8.

SMOTHERED GREENS

Just about everybody in New Orleans has a country cousin—and the most useful thing this cousin can do sometimes is teach the city dweller how to make a meal out of collard, mustard, turnip, or any other pot of greens. Don't toss out the cooking liquid, known as "pot likker"—you sip that like soup between bites of corn bread. ⊘

7 lb (3 kg) greens, one variety or mixed
$3/4$ lb (340 g) lean bacon, cut in cubes
1 cup (170 g) finely chopped onion
$1/2$ cup (60 g) chopped celery
$3/4$ cup (110 g) chopped green bell pepper (capsicum)
2 lb (1 kg) ham hocks
Salt and black pepper
Black pepper to taste
2 tablespoons white vinegar
Hot peppered vinegar

Use only the tender leaves of the washed greens, breaking them into 2-in (5-cm) pieces. Cook the bacon in a heavy kettle until the fat is rendered, then add the onion, celery, and bell pepper. Stir over medium heat for about 5 minutes, then add the greens. Cover and cook until the greens are wilted, about 15 minutes.

Add the ham hocks, salt and pepper to taste, and vinegar. Cover and cook for another 15 minutes. Then pour in 2 cups (500 ml) of water, cover, and simmer for 90 minutes. Serve with a bottle of hot peppered vinegar for additional heat. Serves 10.

DIRTY RICE

Chef Greg Picolo, The Bistro

The livers of chickens lend their color to this rice dish, making it appear "dirty." ①①

2 cups (400 g) uncooked long-grain rice
1 large onion, finely chopped
1 green bell pepper (capsicum), finely chopped
2 tablespoons minced garlic
2 celery ribs, finely chopped
2 tablespoons butter
2 tablespoons Worcestershire sauce
1 duck or chicken liver, chopped coarsely
1/2 lb (225 g) ground beef
1 cup (250 ml) Marsala or Madeira
2 cups (500 ml) Beef Stock (page 41)
1 rounded tablespoon dried tarragon
4 tablespoons unsalted butter
1 teaspoon ground red pepper (cayenne)

In a medium-sized saucepan, combine the rice with 4 cups water. Cover and bring to a boil, then reduce the heat and boil gently until just tender, 10 to 12 minutes. Drain, rinse, and set aside.

In a large skillet, sauté the vegetables in the 2 table-spoons butter until soft, then add the liver, ground beef, and Marsala. Add the beef stock and Worcestershire sauce, cooking 3 minutes. Then add precooked rice and finish cooking, until the liquid is absorbed. Stir in the unsalted butter and red pepper. Serves 6.

BLACK-EYED PEAS

With the rest of the South, New Orleans loves black-eyed peas. Though the following recipe is prepared year-round, it's cooked in most homes for New Year's Day, as tradition holds it will bring good luck in the 364 days that lie ahead. ①

2 lb (1 kg) dried black-eyed peas
1/2 lb (225 g) lean bacon, cut into 1/4-in (6-mm) cubes
1 green bell pepper (capsicum), chopped
1/2 cup (90 g) chopped onion
1/2 cup (110 g) chopped celery
2 teaspoons red wine vinegar
3 cups (750 ml) Chicken Stock (page 40)
Salt and black pepper

Rinse and drain the black-eyed peas; set aside. Brown the bacon in a heavy kettle and add the chopped pepper, onion, and celery. Cook until wilted, stirring often, about 3 minutes. Add the peas, vinegar, and stock, season to taste with salt and pepper and bring to a boil. Cover and let simmer for 1 hour.

Add 5 cups (1 1/4 liters) of water, return to a boil, and let simmer for an additional hour. Stir from the bottom, check the peas occasionally and, if necessary, add additional hot water. Serves 16 to 20 as a vegetable, about 10 over white rice as a main dish.

CHICKEN CREOLE

The old Creoles took the basic chicken fricassee and made it something all their own. Served with white rice, it makes a colorful and satisfying family-style dinner. ⏱

2 3-lb (1½-kg) fryers, cut into 6 pieces
Salt and black pepper
⅓ cup (80 ml) plus 1 tablespoon all-purpose (plain) flour
Vegetable oil
1 tablespoon vegetable oil
1 large onion, finely chopped
1 large green bell pepper (capsicum), finely chopped
2 garlic cloves, minced
2 parsley sprigs, minced
2 celery ribs, finely chopped
1 teaspoon dried thyme
1 bay leaf
1 large tomato, chopped
2 cups (500 ml) water
Hot cooked white rice

Season the chicken pieces with salt and pepper and dust with flour. Cover the bottom of a large heavy skillet with oil and brown the chicken pieces. Remove from the skillet and drain on absorbent paper.

In a saucepan, make a roux by stirring together the additional 1 tablespoon each of oil and flour, cooking over medium heat until dark brown, 10 to 15 minutes. Add all remaining ingredients, except the cooked rice, and stir the mixture at a simmer until it thickens, about 20 minutes. Add the browned chicken and simmer until it is tender, about 1 hour. Taste and add salt and pepper as needed. Serve with white rice. Serves 6.

CRÈME BRÛLÉE

Photograph on page 121

6 egg yolks
⅓ cup (70 g) white sugar
2½ cups (625 ml) heavy cream
1 tablespoon vanilla extract
3 tablespoons dark brown sugar

Preheat the oven to 250°F (120°C, gas mark ½). Using a mixer at medium speed, beat the egg yolks and white sugar in a bowl. Set aside. In a pan, bring the cream to a boil, remove from heat and add it to the egg-sugar mixture, beating the entire time. Add the vanilla. Continue to beat until the mixture is cool. Pour into 6 4-fl oz (125-ml) custard cups.

Place the custard cups in the pan. Add water until it reaches halfway up the sides of the cups. Bake for 50 minutes, then remove the cups from the pan, allow to cool at room temperature and refrigerate until chilled.

Evenly spread about ½ tablespoon of brown sugar over the mixture in each cup. Set the cups on a sheet pan lined with parchment paper and set under a preheated broiler until the sugar melts, darkens, and forms a crust. Watch very carefully and don't allow the sugar to scorch. Refrigerate until ready to serve. Serves 6.

Sources of Ingredients

The ingredients used in this book are frequently found in supermarkets or specialty food stores all over. Ingredients not found locally may be available from the suppliers listed below.

A Gourmet Cajun Shop, LLC
18592 Perkins Road
Prairieville LA 70769
Tel: (225) 313-6041
cajun-shop.com
bigeasy@cajun-shop.com

Bubba's Produce Co.
Wholesale Produce
400 Marigny Street
New Orleans, LA
Tel: (504) 949-2112

Café du Monde Coffee Shop
800 Decatur Street
New Orleans, LA 70116
Tel: (800) 772-2927
cafedumonde.com

Carriage Foods
2437 Delaware Ave
Kenner, LA 70062
Tel: (504) 466-9391

Comeaux's
116 Alley 3
Lafayette, LA 70506
Tel: (888) 264-5460
comeaux.com

Creole & Cajun Cuisine
Tel: (337) 509-0515
creoleandcajun.com
info@creoleandcajun.com

Creole Country Sausage Factory
512 David Street
New Orleans, LA 70119
Tel: (504) 488-1263

Creole Delicacies, Inc
533 St. Ann Street
New Orleans, LA 70116
Tel: (504) 523-6425
cookincaju.com

Gumbo Ya-Ya
600 Decatur St
New Orleans, LA 70130
gumbonola.com

Inland Seafood Inc
2527 Perdido St
New Orleans, LA 70119
inlandseafood.com

Louisiana Seafood Exchange
428 Jefferson Highway
Jefferson, LA 70121
Tel: (504) 834-9393
louisianafoodexchange.net

Magic Seasoning Blends
720 Distributors Row
New Orleans, LA 70123
Tel: (504) 731-3590
magicseasoningblends.com

New Orleans School of Cooking
524 St. Louis St
New Orleans, LA 70130
Tel: (504) 525-2665
neworleansschoolofcooking.com

Pure Cajun Products
Tel: (504) 273-5137
purecajun.com
purecajun@purecajun.com

Reily Foods Company
400 Poydras St, 10th Floor
New Orleans, LA 70130
reilyproducts.com
service@reilyproducts.com

Shopping Guide

The beautiful props and art shown throughout this book come from shops in New Orleans and its vicinity. The numbers in italics at the end of each entry indicate page numbers.

Adler's (722 Canal Street) has defined New Orleans style for nearly a hundred years. Coleman E. Adler established the family jewelry business in 1898 on Royal Street in the French Quarter and quickly gained a reputation for excellence in the sale of fine jewels. Adler's moved to its present location on Canal Street in 1904. Today a fourth generation of the Adler family is bringing together a selection of the finest jewelry, watches, china, crystal, and silver. *43; 47; 57 crab forks; 59 platter; 61; 71 soup bowl; 73 bowl and spoons; 79 plates; 89 napkins and glass; 91 platter; 93 ramekin and fork; 95; 97 plate; 101; 103 cutlery; 107; 111 glass; 115 plate; 117; 119 glass; 121 plate; 123; 131 glasses; 132 napkin.*

Animal Art (617 Chartres Street) specializes in fine antiques depicting animals. Owner Charles Murphy's unusual wares include furniture, screens, paintings, Palissy, Massier ceramics, majolica, faience, painted furniture, horn furniture, decorative antiques and eccentricities, not to mention beautiful oyster plates such as those that appear on pages 57–59.

Antiques and Things (2855 Magazine Street) bas a wonderfully eclectic array of collectibles in addition to its food-related objects. *103; platter 119.*

Lucullus (610 Chartres Street), named for the Roman general known for his love of feasting, is an unusual French Quarter shop specializing in culinary antiques. Its collection includes European antiques from the seventeenth, eighteenth, and nineteenth centuries, and every object depicts or complements the grand pursuit of gastronomy. Lucullus has an amazing variety of glassware, silver, and porcelain, beautifully displayed on antique tables and buffets. *28; 51; 77 pot, slotted spoon, and bowls; 81 place settings, pot, and chairs; 83 pewter plates; 85 serving dish, 89 charger; 109; 113 picnic set, 129 plate.*

Meyer the Hatter (120 St. Charles Avenue), established in 1894, is still run by members of the family that founded it. Meyer's has a large selection of hats and caps from makers like Stetson, Dobbs, and Borsalino. *121*

So Forth (Canal Place and 701A Dante Street) could also be called *go forth* because when stylist and collector Pamela Benham Kraus sought rare or unusual gift items she usually had to search far and wide. Now these two shops hold her spoils. Showcasing items that are quirky and luxurious, So Forth offers a unique selection of the best things: fine linens, dinnerware, paintings, and distinctive clothing. *57 plates, jug, and vase; 61 napkin; 67 salt and pepper shakers; 69; 73 napkin; 75 bowls; 91 plates and napkin.*

Tezcuco Antiques (Tezcuco Plantation, 3138 Highway 44) was a lovely antique shop at the Tezcuco Plantation. Unfortunately, Tezcuco Plantation was completely destroyed by fire in May 2002. *65 table settting; 81 table, 127.*

On Location

All photos in this book were shot on location in the Crescent City and its environs. Photographs of dishes from particular restaurants were all shot on location in those restaurants.

Bay Tree Plantation's (3785 Highway 18, Vacherie) manor is a French Creole cottage built in the 1850s by Edmond Trepagnier. Each room of this elegant bed and breakfast is decorated with antiques. Hosts Dinah and Rich Laurich offer their guests a full Southern breakfast and charming Southern hospitality. *99*

The Cabin (5405 Highway 44, Gonzales). The Cabin restaurant is one of the ten original slave dwellings of the Monroe Plantation and is over 150 years old. *83, 125*

Houmas House and Gardens (40136 Highway 942, Burnside) are onland along the Mississippi that was purchased from the Houmas Indians in colonial times. The rear house was built in the late 1700s. The magnificent Greek Revival mansion was built in 1840 by John Smith Preston and his wife, Caroline. The Prestons sold the house in 1858 to John Burnside, under whose management the plantations 20,000 acres of sugar cane flourished. The house was lovingly restored to its 1840 splendor by Dr. George B. Crozat in 1940. *28*

Laura Plantation (2247 Highway 18) at Vacherie, is a West Indies-style plantation home built in 1805 by Guillaume Duparc. Six of the original slave quarters and outbuildings are still there today. The plantation is best known for being where the Br'er Rabbit stories (on which Joel Chandler Harris based his Uncle Remus books) are said to have been first told in the United States by Senegalese slaves. *85, 93*

Hotel Maison de Ville and Audubon Cottages (727 Toulouse Street) is a luxurious European-style hotel dating from 1742, and its lovely rooms retain the elegance of that time. The hotel is decorated with fine French antiques and has a palm-tree courtyard in which Tennessee Williams (only one of the hotel's many famous guests) reworked *A Streetcar Named Desire*. The seven Audubon cottages are named for the famed naturalist who lived in cottage number one with his family in the early 1800s. *38, 43, 49*

Nottoway Plantation Resort (31025 Highway 1 at White Castle) is another example of classic Greek Revival architecture and beautiful furnishings. The mansion, built between 1849 and 1859 by Virginian sugar planter John Hampton Randolph, is one of the most opulent on the Mississippi river and is a National Historic Landmark. With over 53,000 square feet, it's the largest antebellum house in the South. There are guided tours, a gift shop, and a restaurant. *129*

Oak Alley Plantation (on Highway 18, Vacherie) is named for its stately alley of twenty-eight oaks that date from the early 1700s. The house was built in 1837 by Jacques T. Roman, and the location has inspired more than a few location scouts—the films *Hush, Hush Sweet Charlotte*, starring Bette Davis, and *Interview with the Vampire* were both filmed there. The plantation has a café, gift shop, and overnight cabins. *113*

The Anne Rice Garden is the garden of Anne Rice's private residence at First and Chestnut in the Garden District. It is not open to the public on a daily basis, but occasional visits are arranged by the author's new company, Anne Rices Very Own New Orleans Tours. *123*

Tezcuco Plantation (3138 Highway 44, Darrow) was listed on the National Register of Historic Places, and was delisted in 2019 (it burnt down in May 2002). This former Greek Revival cottage's main floor sits above a high basement, a style borrowed from French Colonial houses. There was a gift shop, an antiques shop, a café and overnight cabins. *81*

Restaurant Guide

Abita Brewpub
72011 Holly St.,
Abita Springs, LA 70420
(504) 892-5837
abitabrewpub.com

Andrea's Restaurant
3100 19th St., Metairie
LA 70002
(504) 834-8583
andreasrestaurant.com

Antoine's Restaurant
713 St. Louis St.,
New Orleans, LA 70130
(504) 581-4422
antoines.com

Arnaud's
813 Bienville St.
New Orleans, LA 70112
(504) 523-5433
arnaudsrestaurant.com

Bayona
430 Dauphine Street
New Orleans, LA 70112
(504) 525-4455
bayona.com

Bistreaux at Maison Dupuy
1001 Toulouse St.,
New Orleans, LA 70112
(504) 522-8800
maisondupuy.com/dining.html

Brennan's
417 Royal St.,
New Orleans, LA 70130
(504) 525-9711
brennansneworleans.com

Brigtsen's Restaurant
723 Dante St.,
New Orleans, LA 70118
(504) 861-7610
brigtsens.com

The Cabin Restaurant
5405 Highway 44,
Gonzales, LA 70737
(225) 473-3007
thecabinrestaurant.com

Commander's Palace
1403 Washington Ave.
New Orleans, LA 70130
(504) 899-8221
exploretock.com

Emeril's New Orleans
800 Tchoupitoulas St.
New Orleans, LA 70130
(504) 528-9393
emerilsrestaurants.com

Gabrielle Restaurant
2441 Orleans Ave.
New Orleans, LA 70119
(504) 603-2344
gabriellerestaurant.com

Galatoire's
209 Bourbon St.,
New Orleans, LA 70130
(504) 525-2021
galatoires.com

Grill Room (Windsor Court Hotel)
300 Gravier St.,
New Orleans, LA 70130
(504) 522-1992
windsorcourthotel.com/dining/the-grill-room/

K-Paul's Louisiana Kitchen
416 Chartres St.,
New Orleans, LA 70130
(504) 596-2530
kpauls.com

Palace Cafe
605 Canal St.,
New Orleans, LA 70130
(504) 523-1661
palace.com

Upperline Restaurant
1413 Upperline St.,
New Orleans, LA 70115
(504) 891-9822
upperline.com

Contributors

Marcelle Bienvenu was born in St. Martinville, Louisiana, into a large Acadian family for whom good cooking was almost as great an article of faith as Roman Catholicism. She writes a regular food column, "Cooking Creole" for the *Times-Picayune* in New Orleans and also edited the 1987 edition of *The Picayune's Creole Cook Book,* originally published in 1901.

Syndey Byrd is a New Orleans photographer who specializes in capturing the local culture. Her pictures of subjects as diverse as Carnival krewes, Mardi Gras Indians, and artists at the Jazz and Heritage Festival have been shown across the United States.

Ella Brennan entered the restaurant business to work with her late brother Owen, founder of Brennan's in the French Quarter. Since then, she has served as matriarch to a family of restaurateurs, running Commander's Palace, Mr. B's, Bacco, Palace Café, Redfish Grill (all in New Orleans), and also Brennan's of Houston.

New Orleans native **John DeMers** is the author of thirteen books including *Arnaud's Creole Cookbook* and *The Best Wining and Dining in New Orleans.* A former food editor for United Press International, DeMers is editor and publisher of *EasyFood* and *CoastFood,* both regional food and wine magazines. He is food editor for *New Orleans* magazine and for WYES-TV's weekly program "Steppin' Out."

Paul A. Greenberg is a New Orleans-based freelance writer who settled into his calling after more than twenty years in hotel and restaurant management. He is a frequent contributor to the New Orleans *Times-Picayune,* as well as to business publications around the country.

New Orleans-born **Errol Laborde** is editor of both *New Orleans* and *Louisiana Life* magazines. He is the author of *Mardi Gras: A Celebration.* His "Streetcar" column has been honored with several awards and has been collected and published in two volumes.

Photographer **John Hay** is based in Melbourne, Australia, and holds a bachelor of arts degree in photography from the Royal Melbourne Institute of Technology. He has been a freelance photographer since 1979, specializing in food photography. His credits include eighteen cookbooks, and he is a frequent contributor to *Australian Gourmet Traveller.*

Honey Naylor is a regular contributor to the Fodor's travel guide series. She has made her home for many years in the French Quarter. Now, from her home in Ruston in north Louisiana, she visits New Orleans regularly to update her popular guidebooks.

Index